CLASSIC WALKS IN THE
Lake District

by Walt Unsworth

The Oxford Illustrated Press

© 1988, Walt Unsworth

ISBN 0 946609 50 0

Published by:
The Oxford Illustrated Press Limited, Haynes Publishing
Group, Sparkford, Nr Yeovil, Somerset BA22 7JJ, England.
Haynes Publications Inc., 861 Lawrence Drive, Newbury
Park, California 91320, USA.

Printed in England by:
J.H. Haynes & Co Limited, Sparkford, Nr Yeovil, Somerset.

British Library Cataloguing in Publication Data
Unsworth, Walt
    Classic walks in the Lake District.
    1. Cumbria. Lake District–Walkers'
    guides
    I. Title
    914.27'804858
    ISBN 0-946609-50-0

Design by Roger Lightfoot.
All photos by the author unless otherwise stated.

CONTENTS

ACKNOWLEDGEMENTS

My thanks are due to my wife Dorothy who acted as chauffeur on numerous frenetic trips across the district, which were necessary to obtain better pictures or check on some detail. This gave me much greater freedom of action, since I could be dropped off in one valley and picked up in another.

My thanks are also due to my son Duncan who took most of the black and white pictures. This involved a number of trips up from London, several during the frustrating summer of 1987, which was not the best from a photographic point of view. The colour pictures are mostly my own, but sometimes I've done the occasional black and white shot and Duncan the occasional colour.

Walt Unsworth

INTRODUCTION

The English Lake District

The English Lake District, usually known as Lakeland or simply 'The Lakes', is a mountainous region in the extreme north-west of England. Until the county boundaries were changed in 1974, the area was shared by Cumberland, Westmorland and Lancashire which met at a common boundary on the Wrynose Pass marked by the Three Shire Stone. Since that date, however, Lakeland has been entirely within the new county of Cumbria, the northern limit of which is the Solway Firth and the southern limit the Silverdale peninsula, which it shares with Lancashire.

The Viking invaders came to Cumbria in about 910 AD and unlike the Anglo-Saxons who settled mostly on the fertile fringes of the area such as the Kent valley, had no compunction about pushing into the mountainous interior, clearing the scrub and the glacial boulders and settling in the valley heads. Their names are everywhere and they left us words which are still in use in the area—a valley is a *dale* from the Norse *dal*, and a mountain is a *fell*, from *fjeld*. Thus mountain walking or hill walking is here known as fell walking.

In pre-metric days a mountain in Britain was reckoned to be a hill which exceeded 2000ft (610m); since metrication the generally accepted standard is 600m (1968ft), although there's no hard and fast rule. On this score there are 145 mountains in the Lake District—that is summits which require at least 30m (100ft) of re-ascent from any other summit. There are scores more which are 600m high but don't meet the criterion—including some quite well-known little peaks, like Cofa Pike on the St Sunday Crag ridge (see Walk 36). The highest summit of all is Scafell Pike (3209ft, 978m) in the heart of the region and the lowest 'mountain' is Black Combe at exactly 600m (1986ft); an isolated fell near the southern coast.

Although everyone likes to climb the highest fells, 'because they are there', height is not the only means of judging a mountain. Form comes into it too: for example, Blencathra in the northern fells is 207ft (63m) lower than its neighbour Skiddaw, but Blencathra *looks* a better mountain and is a finer climb. Obviously, shape matters, and since the shape is largely determined by the geology, the geology matters too.

For our purposes, thank goodness, there's no need to go into the complex geology in detail. All we need to know is why the mountains are shaped as they are, why Skiddaw is lumpy and rounded whereas Gable is spiky and sharp.

Different Sorts of Rock

In very general terms there are three bands of rock across the fells. From north to south these are the very old Skiddaw slates, the slightly younger Borrowdale volcanics and the younger still Silurian slates. The time span for these three is roughly 500 million to 400 million years ago. Surrounding these on the north, east and south is a band of limestone and some coal measures, and in the east, north and west, new red sandstone. There are smaller areas of other rock—granite at Shap and in Eskdale, for instance, and even gabbro on Carrock Fell (which accounts for the only half-decent crags in the far northern fells!)

The Skiddaw slates are not slates at all really but a sort of mudstone. It breaks down into small flakes so that the crags are quite useless for climbing, being too friable and the mountains themselves are easily reduced by erosion to rounded summits. Skiddaw itself is the most obvious example, but the Grasmoor and Robinson groups are others. The limit of these fells is roughly the southern end of Derwent Water. Curiously, there is a separate little area of Skiddaw slate in the south at Black Combe—another rounded fell.

The Borrowdale Volcanics are hard, sharp rocks which do not weather easily. They form a broad central band from Derwent Water down to the northern end of Windermere and Coniston. These are the rocks which typify the Lake District to the visitor; the ones giving rise to exciting mountain shapes like Great Gable and the Langdale Pikes, or gaunt climbing crags like Scafell.

South of this the district is founded on rocks of the Silurian period, which erode more than the Borrowdale volcanics but not quite as much as the Skiddaw rocks. The consequence is the lumpy but generally low fells like those between Coniston and Windermere. From about Kendal southwards these rocks are capped by limestone giving rise to Whitbarrow, Farleton and the Silverdale rocks, which give lovely short walks (see Walks 1–4). In the north, limestone also occurs and gives us the Howk (Walk 40).

All these rocks were sculpted by massive ice flows during the Ice Age; grinding, scraping, plucking, dumping drumlins and erratic boulders, scooping out dales and leaving sharp ridges. The ice advanced and retreated three times. It came first about 210,000 years ago, returned 130,000 years ago and finally 55,000 years ago. This last visitation was with us until 8,000 years ago, and it was the least extensive of the three. In between there were relatively warm periods, like the one we are in now—so the ice may well come back.

One final point about the geology—in amongst the massive rocks were veins and loads of minerals like copper and lead and commercial slate of high quality. These have been responsible for much of the area's prosperity over the years. Even Neolithic man discovered a hard volcanic tuff which flaked and could be shaped into axes, which found their way even as far as the Continent — probably Britain's first export industry!

The Spokes of a Wheel

In 1792 Captain Joseph Budworth strode through the English Lake District setting a fashion which has persisted and grown to the present day. He was the first fellwalker. It is true that others had admired the splendid scenery before the good captain came along, but they had done so from a distance. Despite his one arm (he had lost the other at the siege of Gibraltar) Budworth was a man of action and he realised instinctively that the Lakeland hills were not just for looking at but for exploring. He climbed Helm Crag, Skiddaw, Helvellyn, Coniston Old Man and the Langdale Pikes.

Shortly after this William Wordsworth and the other Lake poets began to draw people's attention to the beauty of the area. They too liked to walk the fells. Coleridge made a fellwalking tour with Wordsworth in 1799 and a much more daring one by himself in 1802, during which he descended the dangerous Broad Stand on Scafell; a tricky place of nastily sloping ledges which gave the poet quite a fright.

In 1810 Wordsworth wrote a guidebook to the Lake District in which he likened the valleys to the spokes of a wheel—an analogy so apt that it has been used by most other writers to this day.

'Let us suppose our station to be a cloud hanging midway between these two mountains, at not more than half a mile's distance from the summit of each, and not many yards above their highest elevation,' he wrote, referring to Gable and Scafell, 'we shall then see stretched at our feet a number of valleys, not fewer than eight, diverging from the point, on which we are supposed to stand, like spokes from the nave of a wheel.'

Wordsworth did admit that the analogy was a bit shaky on the eastern side of the district—nevertheless, this wheel-like structure preserved the Lake District from the worst invasions of the nineteenth and twentieth centuries. The high mountain ridges separating the valleys and meeting at the central hub made things very difficult for the railway and road engineers. Only a few narrow mountain passes tackle the steep slopes between valley heads, and some of these have been surfaced within living memory. Only one major road travels through the area from north to south—from Keswick through Ambleside to Kendal— but there are no major east–west roads except at the far northern and southern ends (NB. Not all the A-class roads can be regarded as major roads). From my home south of Kendal it takes almost as long to reach Wasdale by car as it does to reach Newcastle, on the other side of the country! The mountains act as efficient barriers to all but the walkers.

The railway engineers, always more daring than road builders, never succeeded in penetrating the high fells. They could have done it—compared with those faced by Swiss railways the Lakeland fells were small problems—but the expense would not have been justified. Instead, they pushed branch lines to Windermere, Coniston, Lakeside and Boot in Eskdale, of which only the first and last still exist as mainline connections, though the old Lakeside line runs steam excursions from Haverthwaite. The Windermere line should have continued to Ambleside, but Wordsworth and others put a stop to *that* nonsense, and Canon Rawnsley, one of the founders of the National Trust, stopped a branch line being pushed up Borrowdale from Keswick. The idea of extending the Eskdale railway to the summit of Scafell Pike came to nothing too, thank goodness!

In the old days goods travelled by pack-horse across the high passes and there are many such trails through the fells. Some are called 'corpse roads' because deceased dalesfolk were carried along them for burial in the nearest churchyard. There's a well-known one over Burnmoor leading to St Catherine's Church in Eskdale. Some of these old pack-horse roads—tracks, really—are popular walks today, like the Garburn Pass between Kentmere and Troutbeck or Moses Trod between Honister and Wasdale.

The larger lakes, too, offered easy transport in earlier times. Copper ore was shipped down Coniston Water to Greenodd and across Derwent Water to Keswick. Nowadays the 'steamers' (diesel or petrol motor vessels really) operate for passengers on Windermere, Coniston, Derwent Water and Ullswater. For anyone who doesn't fancy the ascent of Place Fell, for example, the trip by steamer to Howtown from Glenridding, with a walk back along the lake shore, makes one of the finest day's outings in the Lake District (see Walk 38).

Windermere (with Bowness) in the south of the area, Ambleside in the centre and Keswick in the north are the three most important centres for tourism and they are all on the main north–south road mentioned earlier. These have every facility, as the brochures say, including good transport to other areas, but there are some delightful smaller places—Patterdale, Coniston, Grasmere, for example—which offer good walking. Some valley heads are noted centres though they have only one or two hotels—the Old and New Dungeon Ghyll Hotels in Langdale, for instance, or the Wasdale Head Inn.

There is so much accommodation in the Lake District that it is quite possible to organise a walking tour, moving from place to place, carrying just a few simple necessities in a rucksack. Such a tour can be based on hotels, farmhouses, youth hostels or camp sites. It is the best way of all of seeing the district, but you need to book each night well in advance, especially if a Bank Holiday is involved and—consider carefully, if you are new to walking—you must push on each day, irrespective of the weather.

Familiar Sights

Every valley of the Lakes has something different and it would be impossible to give even a synopsis in the space available. The story of the dales is told in *An Illustrated Companion into Lakeland* (Oxford Illustrated Press) but there are some things which every walker sees and wonders about—take the famous drystone walls, for instance.

The drystone walls of the Lake District were mostly built between 1750 and 1850, the time of enclosures, and particularly after 1801, the date of the first General Enclosure Act. Some few, such as parish boundary walls, are older. They mark off fields in the valleys, intake land (specially noticeable) and areas of high fell. The latter walls are quite amazing, seeming to run for miles across the most inhospitable and apparently inaccessible country! Sometimes the walls were made specially broad to use up stones littering the fields—there are notable examples of this in Wasdale. They are called drystone because no mortar is used in their construction.

Professional gangs of wallers were employed. They made two parallel rows of footing stones set well in the earth and then built on these, infilling the space between with rubble, called 'hearting'. After every so many courses, through-stones were laid to tie the wall together and stop it from 'bellying'. As it rose in height the wall grew narrower, the slope being known as the 'batter' and a row of cam-stones rested edgewise on top to finish it off. The courses of a good wall are horizontal even when the ground slopes.

Walls can have hogg-holes to let sheep get from one field to the next. Sometimes a distinct break can be seen where the waller has stopped and started again and this usually indicates a change of ownership and therefore upkeep. Though field stones were used whenever possible many of the small quarries seen on the fells were originally opened to provide material for walls. A good waller chose his stones with care, especially the footings, throughs and cam-stones.

The farmhouses of the Lake District seem to grow out of the very landscape. Often they are of the longhouse type, where the door is off centre, the larger portion being the house and the shorter portion the down-house, separated by a hallway, or hallan, which ran straight from the front door through to the back. Many were later modified though the basic plan is still apparent. Sometimes the eaves came down over an open gallery traditionally known as a 'spinning gallery', though more likely used for stacking logs out of the wet! Such galleries can be seen at Low Hartsop, Patterdale and Yew Tree Farm near Coniston, amongst other places. Another feature is the bank barn, so easily made in an area where steep slopes are common. A bank barn is built into a slope so that entrance to the lower floor is at the front and entrance to the upper floor at the back, where the ground is higher.

Around the farm are the meadows (not all farms are so lucky!), the inbye land, the intake land and the open fell. There may be some cattle but sheep predominate. At one time it was the hardy Herdwick, dark-fleeced and good at keeping to her own heaf or patch of fell, but now only about 10 per cent are Herdwicks. Over half the flocks now are Swaledales, with Rough Fell and other breeds making up the rest. They are brought down off the heaf for lambing, dipping, shearing and 'tupping'.

Two other features of the fells soon become apparent to a walker—the quarries and the forests. Slate has been a major industry for many years and is currently undergoing something of a boom. Nevertheless there are many abandoned quarries, some of considerable size, like those at Tilberthwaite, near Coniston. Forestry, of the kind practiced by the Forestry Commission—more or less parallel rows of conifers—began in 1919 near Keswick and there are now four major forests at Thornthwaite, Ennerdale, Blengdale and Grizedale. There are two visitor centres at Whinlatter Pass near Keswick and at Grizedale near Hawkshead. The latter includes the well-known Theatre in the Forest, and has recently been extensively modernised. Although the Commission provides walks and nature trails, afforestation, along with reservoir building, has been a major cause of dissension in the Lake District. The lovely Ashstead Fell is about to be forested (see Walk 5).

The National Park

The whole of the central fells, from Caldbeck in the north to the River Kent in the south and from Askham in the east to Ravenglass in the west—880 square miles—was designated a National Park in 1951. It is administered by the Lake District Special Planning Board who look after planning permissions and tourist facilities in the area. They own very little of the land themselves. The biggest landowner is the National Trust which owns or leases more than a quarter of the area in the park. The National Park has information offices throughout the region and a visitor centre at Brockhole, on Windermere. National Trust Land Rovers are a common feature of the summer scene in the Lakes, usually parked at some well-known tourist haunt, offering membership of this voluntary body.

Walking in the Lakes

Lakeland fells offer the same challenge today as they did to Budworth or Coleridge and this alone would attract walkers, but added to that is the incredible beauty of the place. No other region has quite such perfection of form and colouring as the Lake District. Mountains, water and trees blend together in supreme harmony. Even if you are not tempted to walk the high fells, you cannot resist the lure of the riverside and the woods. The walks in this book cater for all tastes. They are not aimed at the long-distance walker but at the average family. Some walks are more strenuous than others, of course, but there's nothing in this book that a reasonably active family cannot attempt on a good summer's day. At the same time, common sense is needed: it would be extremely foolish to choose one of the harder walks if you or your companions had not done any mountain walking before. Much better to build up to it by starting with something simple like Cats Bells or Loughrigg.

The four sheets of the Ordnance Survey Outdoor Leisure Map *The English Lakes* at a scale of 1:25,000 are by far the most suitable maps for walking in the Lake District. The book starts with a few walks on the southern fringe of the area and ends with one on the northern fringe; this allows some beautiful walks to be included which are too often ignored. They also often enjoy good weather when the high fells are in cloud.

Although some winter pictures are included in this book for variety, all the descriptions refer to summer. In a good year this can be taken as being from the beginning of May to the end of October. When there's snow and ice about conditions in the high fells may demand mountaineering skills and equipment. Daylight hours are shorter in winter, too, and being benighted on the winter fells is not a happy experience. Some of the valley walks, of course, are pretty safe at any time of year and these should be obvious from their descriptions.

Seathwaite, at the head of Borrowdale, is the wettest place in England with over 150 inches (3.8m) of rain a year.

'Doesn't it ever do anything but rain?' an exasperated visitor demanded from a Seathwaite farmer.

'Oh, aye,' he replied. 'Sometimes it snaws.'

But actually it isn't as bad as all that. The central fells do catch more than their fair share but often it is possible to escape the rain by going to the fringe areas like Silverdale or the Eden Valley. Even at Keswick, only eight miles down the valley from Seathwaite, the rainfall is only a third of Seathwaite's.

The worst months for rain, say the statistics, are November, December and January. Personally, I wouldn't trust March, July or August either! In my experience—and ignoring the statistics—the best months are May, June, September, October and February. But weather is weather, and you can't rely on it—I'm writing this on a June evening when it hasn't stopped raining all day!

Gear for Walking

Many of the valley walks described in this book can be done wearing ordinary trainers, but for anything more ambitious a pair of lightweight walking boots are more comfortable. Some walkers like to wear two pairs of socks for comfort but I prefer just one; it is obviously something you have to decide before you buy the boots! Modern lightweight boots, unlike the heavier mountaineering boots, do not need breaking in. Some are made in suede, but if made of leather there is no need for fancy oils to keep them in trim; ordinary wax polish will do just as well.

After foot comfort comes leg comfort and there's no doubt that mountaineering breeches, made in a fine material and not the old-fashioned cords or moleskin, give the greatest freedom. They are not absolutely essential, of course, and for valley walks or short walks I frequently wear the lightweight travel slacks made by people like Rohan and Mountain Equipment. These garments are much tougher than they seem.

Ordinary trousers will do, but jeans are to be avoided because they are usually too tight and they offer little protection against the weather. Some walkers prefer shorts but in the fells the weather can be unpredictable and if shorts are worn then a warmer alternative should be carried in the rucksack. A light sweater and some shell rain-gear—cagoule and overtrousers—can also go in the sack. Unless you have the correct gear for the fells, bad weather can be more than just an uncomfortable inconvenience. It is essential to maintain a steady body temperature; damp and cold can lead to hypothermia which is a serious medical condition.

These are single-day walks sometimes lasting only two or three hours and we are talking of summer remember, so to carry your gear you just need a small rucksack known appropriately as a 'day-sack'. Besides the clothing already mentioned you need a simple first-aid kit and other 'first-aid' items like toilet paper, matches, a torch and a whistle. The whistle is to summon assistance in an emergency—six blasts per minute is the standard emergency call. At night six flashes per minute from the torch means the same thing.

You may wish to carry a packed lunch and a thermos, but in any case some extra food (usually chocolate) should be carried for emergencies. Resist the temptation to gobble it up out of sheer greed along with the sandwiches—you might regret it!

Map and compass—and a knowledge of how to use them—are essential. A Silva-type compass is best because once you have learned how to use it, it becomes a quick and reliable tool. On a clear day you will scarcely ever need the compass in the Lakes because the paths are so well marked nowadays and all the walks in this book keep to paths. However, in mist it is possible to become disorientated and choose the wrong path and the compass can help in this. By orientating the map, too, anyone who doesn't know the district can use map and compass to identify the surrounding peaks.

Notes

1) In the following descriptions reference is frequently made to museums, houses, etc, open to the public. The dates and times of opening vary considerably according to season. Up-to-the-minute information can be had from local tourist offices, of which there are many. They are listed in the telephone directory for Cumbria and North Lancashire under TOURIST INFORMATION.

2) An indication is given of the time required for each walk but this should not be taken too literally. Quite apart from the fact that it takes no account of halts for food, photography or simply admiring the scenery, the time can be affected by the size and fitness of the party, the weather and conditions underfoot.

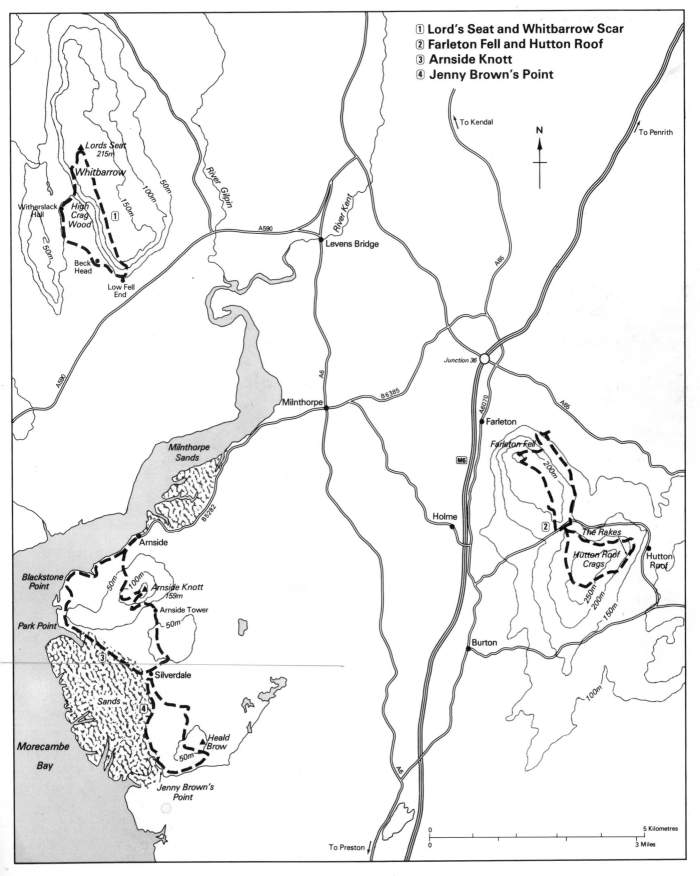

1 Lord's Seat and Whitbarrow Scar
2 Farleton Fell and Hutton Roof
3 Arnside Knott
4 Jenny Brown's Point

To Kendal

N

To Penrith

Lords Seat
215m

Whitbarrow

150m

100m

50m

*High
Crag
Wood*

1

Witherslack
Hall

50m

River Gilpin

River Kent

A590

Levens Bridge

*Beck
Head*

Low Fell
End

A590

A6

A65

Junction 36

Milnthorpe

B6385

A6070

M6

Farleton

Farleton Fell

200m

*Milnthorpe
Sands*

B5282

Holme

2

The Rakes

*Hutton Roof
Crags*

*Hutton
Roof*

Arnside

*Blackstone
Point*

50m

100m

*Arnside Knott
159m*

Arnside Tower

50m

250m

200m

150m

Park Point

3

Burton

100m

Silverdale

Sands

4

*Heald
Brow*

50m

*Morecambe
Bay*

*Jenny Brown's
Point*

A6

0   5 Kilometres

0   3 Miles

To Preston

To Preston

9

WALK 1: Jenny Brown's Point

Map: SD37/47. 1:25,000.
Start: MR456755. Silverdale Cove. Good parking.
Best Access: From the A6 at Milnthorpe via Arnside, or the A6 at Carnforth via Warton and Silverdale. Good navigation required—the Silverdale peninsula is a maze of minor roads! Silverdale is also accessible by rail, with its own station on the Lancaster–Barrow line, about one mile from the village.
Distance: 4 miles (6km). Circular.
Links with other walks: This walk links with Walk 2. Use start for Walk 2.
Time: 2¹/₂ hrs.
What's it Like?: Beautiful limestone coastline with smugglers' coves and extensive views over Morecambe Bay. Virtually no climbing except at Heald Brow which is about 200ft (60m).
Bad weather alternatives: (1) Steamtown Railway Museum, Carnforth, is one of the largest of its kind in the country and the home of *The Flying Scotsman* (496807); (2) Leighton Moss Nature Reserve (Visitor centre 477750). Many varieties of birds, especially waders; (3) Leighton Hall (494744). Home of the Gillow family, of furniture fame.

Above: **The low limestone cliffs of the Silverdale coast**

Part of Britain's Heritage Coast

A purist might argue that the Silverdale peninsula is not actually in the Lake District at all and the southernmost part, which forms this walk, is not even in Cumbria, but Lancashire! All of which is true, but purists, being what they are, never see beyond the statistics. In spirit, this splendid peninsula belongs to the limestone area south of Kendal just as rightfully as Farleton Fell or Whitbarrow. And it adds something which the rest of Cumbria lacks—good coastal walking. Here is

Right: **Warton Crag from Brown's Houses, near Silverdale.**

Far right: **Woodwell, Silverdale.**

some of the most beautiful coastline in Britain.

It forms part of Morecambe Bay's shoreline. The bay is a wide area of very shallow water, famous for its shrimps and flounders. When the tide goes out, the sand stretches as far as the eye can see, with only the Kent Channel cutting its sinuous way through at the northern end, and the Keer Channel at the south. The Kent is reputed to change its channel from the Silverdale side to the Grange side of the estuary, and back again, once in a person's lifetime and this seems to be borne out in the present century. There are photographs showing a pleasure steamer close in to the Silverdale shore in 1905 and now the river is back again, having been for many years on the Arnside bank. Some severe winter storms in 1984 and 1985, coinciding with high tides, accelerated the process.

Silverdale Cove, where our walk begins, is as good a place as any to see the full sweep of the Sands, as they are called. A narrow lane leads down to the cove from the Elmslack road. No doubt this was used by shrimpers to trundle their carts down in the old days, and sometimes cross-sands traffic would come this way instead of the longer journey from Hest Bank, especially if the River Keer was in awkward mood. Low cliffs line the cove and a cave, like the eye of a Cyclops, peers out of one of them. It is a shallow affair, quite safe to explore. On the opposite side of the cove is Red Rake; a distinctive little gully which was a trial working for iron ore, probably for the Leighton furnace about three miles away on Leighton Beck. Iron ore from Furness would be landed at the cove too—and so would other things, for this was a notorious coast for smuggling.

The Sands themselves were for many years used by travellers as a short cut from Lancaster to Furness—eight miles as against thirty via Kendal. A public coach service commenced in 1781 despite the well-known dangers of quicksands, tricky river crossings and an incoming tide which was said to be swifter than the fastest horse. The coaches continued until 1857, when the newly completed railway put them out of business. Though hundreds of people walk across the sands each year, guided by Cedric Robinson the official 'sand-pilot', no further crossings were made by horse and carriage until the Duke of Edinburgh crossed the Sands from the cove to Kent's Bank with a coach and four in 1985.

It is dangerous to try crossing the Sands without a guide and even wandering about on them is not without danger. Several people have to be rescued from quicksands every year.

Out of sight on the cliffs above the cave lies Cove House, at one time the holiday home of the Rev. Carus Wilson, founder of the famous girls' school at Cowan Bridge (now at Casterton), where the Brontë sisters were amongst the earliest pupils.

All this can be seen in a matter of minutes

before turning our steps south along the shore. The sea-washed turf is not as extensive here as it is further north (see Walk 2) but it still exhibits the same characteristics of deep sink-holes filled with water. In a few minutes the curious row of houses known as Shore Cottages is reached. Here is another way down to the beach from the village. A few yards up the lane is the Silverdale Hotel, once an old coaching house called the Britannia.

Our way, however, continues along the shore until a path can be seen on the left which climbs the low cliffs and then runs along the tops of them like a narrow ribbon. It leads first to one small cove and then another as the coast becomes increasingly rocky and romantic. Wind-tortured trees lean against the rocks and on a gusty day, if the tide is in, the surf pounds against the crags and spray is flung high into the air.

Eventually the way leads to an area of broken slabs tilting down into a magnificent rocky cove. The prominent headland on the opposite side of the cove is known as Jack Scout and so this is Jack Scout Cove—though it is better known locally by the strange name of Cow's Mouth. The limestone crags of the headland offer some interesting rock climbs for experts.

If the tide is out it is possible to walk on the sands round the headland to Jenny Brown's Point, but this is less interesting than climbing Jack Scout. To do this it is necessary to go through the stile at the back of the cove and almost immediately turn right up a short scree slope where, hidden by trees, there is a natural break in the rocks, like a miniature Jack's Rake on Pavey Ark. A scramble up this leads to the top of the headland.

Jack Scout belongs to the National Trust as part of the Heritage Coast. A limekiln has been restored and there is a huge limestone bench known as the Giant's Seat which gives wide views over the bay. In the distance can be seen the square tower of Heysham Power Station, a recent addition of the nuclear age, and the domed Ashton Memorial which overlooks Lancaster. Our way leads to the right, following a path round the headland. Eventually it is possible to clamber down to the shore where a curious wall like an old quay can be seen and beyond it, stretching out across the Sands, a long embankment of broken rocks—all that remains of an ambitious nineteenth century scheme to reclaim land in the bay. The scheme foundered through lack of money and the embankment was covered by the Sands—only to reappear in 1977 after a severe storm!

The coast near Jenny Brown's Point. (Photo: Duncan Unsworth).

The old smelter chimney near Brown's houses. (Photo: Duncan Unsworth).

The square pond at Woodwell, one of the wells that served Silverdale for years. (Photo: Duncan Unsworth).

This is Jenny Brown's Point, though who Jenny was is not known. The cottages nearby are called Brown's Houses and the farmhouse—Dyke's Farm—is seventeenth century. The cottages were probably built along with the copper smelter in the early 1790s and the quay we have already passed was built at the same time. All that remains of the smelting works is a gaunt chimney, standing like a lost sentinel on the shore beyond Brown's Houses.

Our way lies past the chimney. The saltings here are broad and heavily populated by sheep, though quite a bit of turf was stripped away recently to make suburban lawns in Surrey— this close-grained sea-washed grass is quite the best lawn turf there is, and the most expensive! You can see it at Wembley and Wimbledon.

Across the saltings can be seen Crag Foot and another chimney. The chimney was part of the pumping scheme which helped drain Leighton Moss but there were also a number of copper mines at Crag Foot which helped feed the smelter at Jenny Brown's Point. There was also the curious paint mine where red iron oxide was dug for making paint and 'red raddle', once a popular polish for doorsteps. The mine is now locked up but I once had the privilege of being taken down it and I can vouch for the permanency of the paint! My old clothes were stained with an immovable red. A friend of mine had a similar experience—he left red footprints on the road near the mine, and they could still be seen months later!

The path can be a bit boggy beyond the chimney but before long an embankment is reached and a sign points up the wooded hillside on the left saying 'Heald Brow & Woodwell'. The path up Heald Brow can only be described as tenuous. It is best to tackle the rather steep slopes by going first right and then left in a large zig-zag. In any case, you want to end up to the left where a slit stile leads to the fields above, and before long a strangely overgrown lane is met which leads to a surfaced road of the minor sort.

Across the road is a sign saying 'Woodwell' and pointing to a path which passes through a wooded glade. On the right are steep rocks and where these at last break free from the trees there is a spring issuing from below a small overhang. On the left a large square pond has been made, now reed-filled. It is a charming spot and the best known of the various wells which served Silverdale for many years. The village did not receive mains water until 1938.

By keeping close in to the crag a few yards beyond the well it is possible to discern a short scramble up the rocks which continues the line of the path. The walk becomes a woodland idyll and leads eventually to Stankelt Road near Silverdale Green. About a quarter of a mile down this road, beyond the junction, where it turns sharply left at Post Office Hill is the Old Post Office and just beyond, a set of steps and a gate leading into the fields beyond which are known as the Post Office Lots. A path leads across the Lots back to Silverdale Cove.

The sands of the Kent Estuary seen from Jenny Brown's Point.

WALK 2: Arnside Knott

Above: **Evening, the Bay from Arnside Knott** (Photo: Duncan Unsworth).

Map: SD37/47. 1:25,000
Start: MR454786. On the promenade at Arnside. Good parking.
Best Access: From the traffic lights at Milnthorpe along the B5282. Arnside has a station on the Lancaster–Barrow railway line. It is at the eastern edge of the village, about half a mile from the start of this walk.
Distance: 7 miles (11km). Circular.
Links with Other Walks: This walk can be combined with Walk 1. Start as above and join Walk 1 at Silverdale Cove. At Stankelt Road do not turn left but go straight across, through some houses and follow a path through the field ahead to St. John's Church. Turn right and follow the road to the junction at Potter Hill. Left here by a clear path to join the bridleway around King William's Hill which runs by a high wall until it picks up Walk 2 at Elmslack. Combined walk, about 12 miles (19km).
Time: 3hrs (Combined walk: 5¹/₂hrs).
What's it Like?: A fine coastal walk with some secluded bays and wonderful views over the Kent estuary. The going can be a bit rough at times. The climb up Arnside Knott is gentle, about 400ft (120m). Good viewpoint for the Lakeland fells and for sunsets over the estuary, which can be spectacular.
Bad Weather Alternatives: See Walk 1. Arnside does not have much to offer for a wet day, despite being a small resort. You could take the train across the estuary to Grange, which is a somewhat bigger resort—but that doesn't have much either!

Fossils and Flowers

Looking across the broad shallows of the Kent estuary today, it is hard to believe that this river was once the only port in the old county of Westmorland. Ships would land their cargoes at Arnside, Sandside and Milnthorpe—coal and iron-ore often as not—

and take on board cloth and snuff from Kendal. It can never have been a big port and no doubt the ships were small in size too, but it was important in the days when roads were often impassable. Kendal and Milnthorpe were great pack-horse centres, where the goods were broken down into manageable parcels and carried into the wild fell country round about.

In less than fifty years the whole thing came to an end. The opening of the Lancaster–Kendal canal in 1819, the new turnpike from Carnforth to Milnthorpe in 1818, the railway to Carlisle in 1846 and Barrow in 1857 and, of course, the increasing size of ships, put an end to Westmorland's port. The railway was simply the final nail in the coffin; the viaduct across the Kent at Arnside prevented ships from sailing up river.

Nowadays, when the tide is in, sailing boats glide across the estuary, their brightly coloured sails adding a touch of tinsel to a glorious setting. For make no mistake about it—this estuary is one of the most beautiful in Britain.

Arnside was a fishing village popularised as a resort by the railway, though always one of a genteel nature. It is the sort of place one imagines elderly ladies writing torrid novels and not at all like that big brash place called

Blackpool just a short distance down the coast. The population is about 1800. Our walk starts at the end of the promenade where there is a concrete walkway leading eventually to the shore.

Once past the coastguard station, bare rock starts to show itself, either natural or quarried and it is worth examining it for fossils. Note the tiny rings of crinoids and the more individual brachiopods. Across the water the quarried crag of Meathop stands out significantly.

Before long the shore walk leads to a broad bay of saltings and sand, dissected by a deep creek. On the opposite side of the bay are some houses, New Barns, and though it is possible to go straight across the bay to them, crossing the creek can be tricky and it is probably as well to walk round. The shore becomes pebbly and sometimes quite painful if you are wearing trainers or thin shoes but it soon improves and before long you come to Blackstone Point, where the coast turns abruptly south. Across the river can be seen Holme Island, Grange-over-Sands, and in the distance the rocky lump of Humphrey Head, one of the many places where the last wolf in England was killed.

At times of high tide it might be difficult to keep to the shore at Blackstone Point, and if

Above: **The view from Arnside Knott. In the foreground are the knotted trees.** (Photo: Duncan Unsworth).

Below: **The sad remnants of the knotted trees on Arnside Knott. In the background is an enclosure holding two replacement saplings which have recently been knotted together.** (Photo: Duncan Unsworth).

16

The viaduct across the Kent at Arnside.

On the shore at Arnside. Across the estuary is Grange-over-Sands.

The Kent Estuary from Arnside Knott.

the wind is blowing strongly from the west, it might even be exciting! The waves come crashing in with all the force of the Irish Sea behind them and it is as well to stay clear—fortunately there is a path on top of the cliffs. If the tide is on the turn as you round the point, you might be lucky enough to see the river bore racing up the estuary, faster than a man can run, or a horse can gallop. Nowadays, the bore hardly ever exceeds 18 inches, but before the building of the railway viaduct at Arnside, the bore could reach $3^1/_2$ feet with a following wind. At high tide the force and direction of the wind can make quite a difference to the water levels. A friend of mine who lives on the banks of the Bela at Milnthorpe (a tributary of the Kent) tells me that a nine-metre tide with a strong west wind will bring the water up to his back doorstep, whereas a ten-metre tide, in calm weather, hardly reaches the foot of his garden.

Around the point there is another bay, White Creek, where the trees crowd to the edge of the cliff and the place seems utterly cut off from civilization. It is hard to realise that just behind those trees is one of the largest caravan sites in the area! But you can't see it, and that is one of the nice things about the Arnside–Silverdale area; despite the proliferation of caravan sites they are all extremely well concealed.

A path runs along the cliff top towards Park Point. On a bright summer's day this stretch of the coast is positively idyllic, with the light glinting off the bay and the estuary and a host of wild flowers at your feet: daffodils and lily of the valley in their seasons and a pretty pink wild geranium. The vista opens up now to include the whole of Morecambe Bay, and, if the tide is out, the great Sands stretching to the horizon.

Soon it is time to leave the cliff-top path and descend to the saltings; the acres of sea-washed turf which fill the wide crescent of Silverdale Bay. The grass is incredibly short and more densely packed than the knots on a Persian carpet. It is hard wearing, yet has a fine almost silky texture, so it is hardly surprising that it is highly prized for making top class lawns. Fortunately at this point it is protected.

At the far side of the bay Silverdale village can be seen; scattered houses on top of the cliffs. The saltings appear to offer a level green path right across, but it isn't long before you discover that this is not the case because the turf is riven by a myriad channels, deep and full of water. It is like walking in a maze, twisting this way and that to get round the channels. Sometimes, out of frustration or bravado, it is tempting to jump across to save the detour. There is no avoiding them, but the best line is found by keeping some way out from the cliffs.

The holes are formed by fresh-water springs emerging from the limestone. The water percolates through the sand, which in time collapses, in a manner not unlike the sink-holes which are so common in limestone areas. Sea-water comes in at high tides, but the saltings are usually only fully covered during the highest of the autumn and spring tides.

After about a mile the Leeds Holiday Camp appears on the cliff top, looking like something from a 1930s travel poster. Its seaward facade is actually quite appealing—which is more than can be said for the stalag-like appearance it shows at the rear! Just beyond here we come to Silverdale Cove (the starting point for Walk 1) and leave the coast.

The next half-mile or so leads along the lanes towards Elmslack. By turning left at the newish looking houses and following your nose towards the woods on the hill ahead, you eventually come into the lane which skirts King William's Hill. This soon peters out by some cottages and a rough track leads through the woods to emerge suddenly in the midst of a large caravan park. In summer this can be a startling experience, emerging almost at a step from the cool quiet woods into a crowded site with families playing football and badminton. In winter it is quite eerie: empty tarmac roads with lonely lamp-posts, like some long-abandoned army camp.

Any prejudice you may have against caravan sites must surely vanish here, for this is beautifully maintained and a model for others. You have to walk across a corner of it, bearing right, to a ladder stile in the perimeter fence. In the field beyond is the best preserved of the local pele-towers, Arnside Tower. Like the other towers in the area Arnside was built as protection against the marauding Scots, especially after the defeat of Edward II at Bannockburn by Robert the Bruce, in 1314. The Scots came in 1316 and 1322 in force—on the second occasion crossing the Sands from Furness to ravage Lancaster.

Arnside Tower was built by the de Broughton family about 1340. It was damaged by fire in 1602 but was restored and inhabited until 1690. From then it has been a sad story of neglect. A corner of the tower was destroyed by storm in 1884 and the ravages of wind and weather have seriously weakened the structure which is no longer in a safe condition.

Above left: **The fine sea-washed turf of the Silverdale coast – but a tricky area to cross.**

Above right: **Silverdale Cove and its cave. At this point the walk turns inland, but it is also the starting point for Walk 1.**

Our walk takes us by the tower, then through the farmyard beyond to the narrow lane leading up to the motor road below Arnside Knott. The position of the pele-tower, guarding the gap between the Knott and Middlebarrow Hill, can be fully appreciated from this point.

Arnside Knott (522ft/159m) looks quite formidable on this side because of the steep shilla slopes—bare limestone scree interspersed with scrub and woodlands. Shilla is a local word for scree. Because of erosion, paths on the shilla slopes are not recommended and it is worth bearing in mind that Arnside Knott is only a little hill, yet it has to bear an inordinate amount of tourist traffic. It would be only too easy to kick it to death.

A National Trust signpost indicates the path we want. It is broad and so well made that it is obviously Victorian. It is known as Saul's Drive and it climbs through the woods and meets a sort of path crossroads where, by following the track leading off right the open crest of the hill is reached at a seat. By turning right here the crest can be followed to the summit, which is a trig block set in a little clearing in the scrub. On the way you pass what remains of the Knotted Trees—two trees which were knotted together as saplings and grew up entwined in a most curious fashion. Age and weather have taken their toll unfortunately and only one tree remains. It doesn't look as though it will stand many more winter gales.

We want to return along the crest, but if time and energy are still abundant it is an interesting diversion to descend from the trig block towards the shilla slopes along a narrow path which tunnels through a dense thicket. Soon this turns right and teeters along the top of the scree, somewhat exposed. There are grand sweeping views over Arnside Tower, Middlebarrow and the bay. With luck the path will return us to the crest at the seat, but path variants are not lacking on Arnside Knott so you need a general sense of direction if you are not to walk round in circles.

Back on the hill crest the path leads to a view indicator, called the Toposcope, which has three panels engraved with the panorama of the Lakeland fells. If it is one of those clear, sharp mornings when visibility stretches to the ends of the earth, the distant view encompasses all the fells from the Pennines and Howgills across High Street and Helvellyn to Coniston Old Man and Black Combe. Even distant Skiddaw can be seen poking its head above Dunmail Raise. Much nearer are the Cartmel fells and in the foreground the magnificent estuary itself. On a fine evening this is the place to enjoy some splendid sunsets, when the bay and the estuary glitter like blood-red tinsel.

Anyone feeling tired at this point will harbour resentment at the discovery that there is a car park only a few steps away from the indicator. The truth is that the summit of the Knott can be reached in a few minutes from stepping out of the car! Nevertheless, the honest walker can affect an air of smug satisfaction in the knowledge of a job well done—and the further knowledge that his own car is only fifteen minutes further.

The road from the car park leads swiftly down to the large convalescent home and on into the village where it turns to the right. Within a few yards a narrow alleyway can be seen sloping steeply down to the shore, the promenade and the car.

WALK 3: Farleton Fell and Hutton Roof

Map: SD57, SD58. 1:25,000.
Start: MR547808. A narrow road on east side of fell. Good parking beyond first gate.
Best Access: From Junction 36 on the M6 via Farleton hamlet.
Distance: 6 miles (10km). Circular.
Time: 3 hrs+.
What's it Like?: Steep 600ft (183m) to start then very little climbing. Wonderful limestone scenery—time can be spent exploring. Suitable for any season, but wet weather or snow would make the limestone dangerous—watch for twisted ankles! Famous views.
NB. Some access problems have recently been reported on the approach to the fell from Farleton lane (1988).
Bad Weather Alternative: Visit Kirkby Lonsdale (about 3 miles (5km) from Hutton Roof). Scenic little town. Good church. Fine walk along River Lune from Devil's Bridge to the Church and Ruskin's View. (30–45mins).

Limestone Hills and Remarkable Rock Scenery

If ever a couple of hills turned their backs on the world then it must be the two little limestone fells which lie on the southern edge of the district between Milnthorpe and Kirkby Lonsdale. Both can be seen from the M6 motorway which runs directly below them and though Hutton Roof can hardly be distinguished—just a low wooded swelling—Farleton is more conspicuous because it resembles a great pudding of shale, fringed by a top-knot of low limestone cliffs. Neither seems in the least attractive.

Yet these two fells encompass some of the most entertaining walking in the district, with unique limestone formations and astonishingly wide-ranging views. Because they are low they can be tackled at any season, though good weather is essential to get the best of the views

Above: **A winter's day on Farleton Fell.**

20

and the limestone can be very slippery in wet weather. A clear crisp day in early spring is ideal.

Of course, each fell could be tackled as a separate walk, most easily from the narrow road which runs between them from Clawthorpe to Hutton Roof hamlet and there is something to be said for this for few places lend themselves so well to just poking around as these hills do—especially Hutton Roof with its romantic jumble of crags, calculated to turn a man's heart back to the wildest dreams of boyhood!

For a first acquaintance, though, an overall impression is what is needed and the walk described here, though it won't reveal all the secrets of this limestone wonderland, gives just that. It starts in a quiet lane near Farleton hamlet where an old green lane leads up to a magnificent limekiln, filled with the rubble of years but otherwise in perfect condition. On the fellside immediately above is the quarry from which, presumably, the limestone for the kiln was extracted. It is fairly big for this sort of undertaking and the kiln must have been a busy one in its heyday. A tenuous path climbs up by the side of the quarry and becomes more certain where it swathes through the bracken to reach a broad bridleway cutting across the hill.

Soon after this the upper crags come into view. In between the land is hummocky, like moraine landscape, but there is a natural broad, low ridge sweeping away to the north towards a cairn. This cairn turns out to be not the highest—that lies immediately above on the left—but one which offers some astonishing views. It is perhaps the finest viewpoint in the entire Lake District—but that's a bold claim in a region which has more good viewpoints to the acre than any other in England.

Away to the north, beyond the vale of the river Kent, the Lakeland fells stretch across the horizon, each group readily identifiable from Coniston to the west to the eastern fells up around Hawes Water. In winter it is a superbly gleaming white barrier, like the distant Alps seen from the Jura. Further east still are the distinctive shapes of the Howgills: magnificent walking country, more rightfully part of the Yorkshire Dales rather than the Lakes, though not similar to either.

The eye sweeps round, past the hills of Dent to the amorphous mass of Gragareth—the highest point in Lancashire since the change in county boundaries robbed the Palatinate of Coniston Old Man! On again to the shapely Ingleborough, standing alone, it seems, on the distant horizon.

The top of the fell is only a short distance away. The view is similar except that now you can see the serried lines of limestone crags which make up the fell. Mostly they are fairly low, fifteen feet or so, but there is one prominent rock wall which reaches three or

Above: **The Rakes, Hutton Roof.**
(Photo: Duncan Unsworth).

Far left: **Uberash Breast: in the wilderness of Hutton Roof.**
(Photo: Duncan Unsworth).

Left: **Winter on Farleton Fell.**
(Photo: Duncan Unsworth).

Farleton Fell seen from Hutton Roof. (Photo: Duncan Unsworth).

four times that height. This is the 'nose' of rock which is such a feature of the fell when seen from the motorway. In fact, despite the prominence of the cairn by which you are standing, the real summit of Farleton Fell lies on top of those crags. A ladder stile in the wall below the crag gives access, should you feel the urge to conquer all!

The route now lies alongside this same wall. It crosses a small saddle and dips down to a bowl in the hillside which has some remarkable limestone formations. It is like an ancient amphitheatre and I once got a celebrated lady publisher, known for her fondness of opera, to give us a few lines from Wagner. This she did *fortissimo*—and scared the life out of a group of fellwalkers who happened innocently on the scene!

One side of this amphitheatre is formed by an enormous glacis of water-worn rock, full of sharp-edged grooves known as karren. Just as rain-water over the centuries has worn away at cracks in the rock to form the grykes, so too rain-water running *on the surface* of the rock forms these distinctive runnels. Farleton Fell and Hutton Roof display this phenomenon on a scale unmatched elsewhere in Britain.

A stile of sorts leads over a fence and the path becomes more distinct. Up on the right is an edge of rock, maybe fifteen feet high. It is worth scrambling up this because it leads to one of the finest limestone pavements in Britain. It is practically level, bare limestone

with a few stunted thorn trees eking out a tenuous existence. Over the entire surface the rock is cracked and fissured by grykes, the deeper ones of which have their own micro-climate harbouring hart's tongue fern and other delicate plants. The whole scene stretches away to the horizon; a sharp white edge drawn against a blue sky.

It is instructive to walk across the pavement, skipping over the grykes, and hoping not to slip and break a leg. It would be mortifying to call out the mountain rescue service on Farleton Fell! When it is wet, limestone can be a slippery sort of rock, so obviously one should keep off the pavement during rainy periods. Instead, it is easy to simply follow the edge round. But all being well, the pavement gives an interesting crossing, especially as there are one or two small cliffs to scramble down *en route*.

The pavement ends suddenly and a path through a field leads to a metalled road, which runs across the fell at this point. Going east along this road for a short way, you come to a sign indicating a path to Hutton Roof, via a stile on the right. The path is broad, easy to follow, but you should watch out for a divergence in a hundred yards—the merest trail leading away to the right towards a line of low crags. By following this you pass, on your left, a wild-looking area of scrub known as Uberash Plain—just one of the many curious names to be found on Hutton Roof. Eventu-

Farleton Fell is one of the best viewpoints for the Lakeland Fells, here seen covered in winter snow.

ally you reach the low crag and by a simple scramble gain an eminence where there are no fewer than three enormous cairns.

Below, to the east, is a remarkable sight: a total chaos of crag and scrub the like of which is hard to match. It looks a fearful place to get embroiled with, and so it is; if you're not careful it will eat you alive. A well-known climber once visited this area out of curiosity, having heard tales about it. Like most people he came in a dismissive frame of mind—after all, Hutton Roof is a very low sort of hill—but before he could escape its clutches, he was benighted and had a tricky time escaping. He still can't figure out how such a little hill can be so difficult . . .

It is best to stay out of the wild interior until you have a greater acquaintance with the fell—though adventurous souls will find this difficult!

A number of prominent landmarks can be identified from our vantage point. The wild jumble of rocks is known as the Potslacks and they gather themselves into a distinct summit with a cairn on top, over in the east (North-East Summit, 876ft (267m). Between that and our present position lies a great whaleback of rock called Uberash Breast which exhibits clints, grykes and karren in profusion. Over to the south-east can just be discerned a trig-block and if you head for this you won't come to much harm, for the going is pretty level and ends at a grassy area where the summit lies at 900ft (274m). The grassy area is called Plover-lands and if you cross it to the north-east you will come upon a grassy valley, hemmed in by a wall on the right and wilderness on the left. A little track runs down the valley. By turning left at a line of crags called the Rakes you will fetch up at a small saddle where there is a curious natural grassy break sweeping down the hill. This has the unusual name of Blasterfoot Gap. On either hand the limestone rises like frozen waves on a seashore. Following the break down leads to an immense perched rock, the Cuckoo Stone, with a bit of a tree sprouting from it, and beyond can be seen the houses of Hutton Roof hamlet.

A broad path leads towards the houses, but this is not our way. Instead, by following the foot of the rocks round to the left, past a limekiln (the second one of the day!) it is possible to return along a good path to the tarmac road between Hutton Roof and Farleton Fell.

At the road junction, a few yards from where you emerge from the fell, there's a concrete lane leading to a farm. The gate is marked Wind Yeats and it is to Wind Yeats that our way now takes us; a long straggle of buildings, but you must watch out for a five-bar gate on the left about half-way through the interminable farm-yard. This leads onto the fell again, but within a hundred yards or so there is a well made diversion off to the right which descends steeply through gorse to emerge by the side of a white house on the little road which curls round the fell. Twenty minutes' walk along this brings you back to the car.

WALK 4: Lord's Seat and Whitbarrow Scar

Above: **A winter day on Whitbarrow and a party of walkers check their bearings.**

Map: SD48 1:25,000.
Start: MR437859. In a lane by Witherslack Hall. Good parking.
Best Access: From the A591 (Kendal by-pass) take the A590 towards Barrow. Turn off right to Witherslack. Go over the crossroads and follow the road ahead for about a mile to the gates of Witherslack Hall. Turn into the lane on the right and park.
Distance: 4$\frac{1}{2}$ miles (7km). Circular.
Time: 2$\frac{1}{2}$hrs.
What's it Like?: A simple walk, short, straightforward and safe with astonishing views rivalling those of Farleton. The ascent and descent are not too steep or arduous.
Bad Weather Alternatives: (1) Levens Hall (495851). Home of the Bagot family, fine Elizabethan mansion with world famous topiary gardens and steam engine collection; (2) Sizergh Castle (498878). Home of the Strickland family for 700 years. Now owned by the National Trust. Fine rock gardens and the home of the National Fern Collection.

A Short Limestone Ridge and an Excellent Viewpoint

The Winster valley is not nearly as well known as its neighbour, the Lyth valley. In summer the latter is busy with traffic seeking an alternative route to Windermere from the south, escaping the busy A591, but the Winster valley has roads which are too narrow for birds of passage: quiet lanes which don't go anywhere in particular but get you there in the end. Until they meet near Crosthwaite, the two valleys are separated by one of the most conspicuous limestone hills in the district, called Whitbarrow, the highest point of which is Lord's Seat (705ft/1215 m). Two sides of this fell, the west and the south, are comprised of sheer limestone crags which rise out of the surrounding woods like something from Conan Doyle's *Lost World*. The southern face is known as White Scar and is partially

Above: **Lord's Seat, Whitbarrow Scar.** (Photo: Duncan Unsworth).

Left: **Chapel Head Scar; the steep crags on the flank of Whitbarrow.** (Photo: Duncan Unsworth).

The view north and west from Lord's Seat. (Photo: Duncan Unsworth).

quarried. This is the face which is so conspicuous from the Barrow road or the A6 at Heversham. Even hardened rock-climbers find this crag intimidating and it has never gained the popularity of nearby Chapel Head Scar.

Chapel Head Scar is the southerly central section of the long west face known collectively as Whitbarrow Scar. In the 1970s it was the scene of a famous dispute between the rock-climbers (who had been over-enthusiastic in stripping away some of the vegetation on the crag) and the naturalists, who didn't want climbing at any price. Eventually the affair was settled more or less amicably, with climbing restricted to certain areas. It is without question the finest limestone climbing crag in the district; exclusively for 'hard men'.

This short walk begins by the gates of Witherslack Hall, which is now a school, but is a place of ancient foundation. It belonged to the Harringtons until they chose the wrong side at Bosworth Field in 1485, when it was given to Sir Thomas Broughton of Broughton

Tower, but two years later he, foolish man, became one of the chief supporters of Lambert Simnel, the impostor who claimed to be king. Broughton was defeated at Stoke in a very bloody battle with Henry Tudor and disappeared. Legend has it that he lived out his life hiding in a cave at Witherslack, looked after by faithful tenants. When he died he was buried in the woods below the crags. The site of his grave was known until the middle of the eighteenth century but has since been lost. Witherslack, along with other Broughton possessions, went to the Stanleys—the family who tipped the balance in Henry Tudor's favour at Bosworth, and placed the crown on the new King's head.

The lane leading towards the scar passes through a stile and then a smaller path leads off it to the left, past the school football field, to enter the woods. There is a signpost at this point, indicating Lord's Seat is to the left, and the path trails pleasantly through the woods to another signpost telling us our way lies upwards. The climb is fairly steep but short

and here and there, through gaps in the all-enveloping greenery, some splendid views can be snatched.

When the path breaks out of the woods it enters a typical limestone upland of bare rock and thin grasses. Cairns lead the way in a wide arc round to the highest point, where there is a substantial cairn with a memorial tablet.

The views from Lord's Seat really are sweeping. To the north the scene embraces the Langdales, the eastern fells, the Howgills, the Dent Fells, Gragareth and Ingleborough. Farleton Fell, nearer than the rest, seems most impressive whilst the view across the Kent estuary to Arnside Knott and Silverdale with the woods and the waters and the sands is quite breathtaking.

The summit is on a strip of land which as old Omar Khayyam once said, 'Just divides the desert from the sown'. One edge is the steep crag plunging down to the Winster valley and the other is a stone wall barring access to a wooded area. This strip, perhaps a couple of hundred yards wide, runs along the length of the scar and our route follows it south along a decent path which goes through a stile and fetches up above the great prow of rock where the west and south faces meet. Looking at these rocks from the Barrow road any sane person would declare them to be a total barrier, and yet there is actually a well-graded path descending them where the woods clothe the limestone and hide its true nature.

The path descends to a bridleway and by following this through the woods, west, then taking to an obvious footpath, we come to the attractive hamlet of Beck Head—aptly named, because there is a stream resurgence here, which you can see by taking a few steps back along the lower road at the junction.

From the junction the top road leads north-west over a shoulder of hill to join the motor road to Witherslack Hall, about half a mile from the gates and the car.

Whitbarrow from the Kent estuary. On the right are the steep crags of White Scar and on the left Beckhouse Wood, where the descent is made.

28

WALK 5: Whinfell Ridge and Borrowdale

Above: **The Whinfell Ridge looking towards Mabbin Crag. In the background are the Howgills in winter garb.**

Map: English Lakes (SE) 1:25,000. This is a most awkward walk for maps, as the last mile or so at the Lune end is missing. Fortunately they are not really necessary, because the route is obvious. However, Wainwright's *Walks on the Howgill Fells and Adjoining Fells* is very useful and can be recommended.

Start: MR551035. A gate a few yards south of the parking place near Huck's Bridge on the A6 about 8 miles (13km) out of Kendal.

Distance: 10 miles (16km). Circular.

Time: 4¹/₂hrs.

What's it Like?: Though the highest point of this walk is only some 1600ft (490m) above sea level, it has all the feel of a high mountain ridge. This is totally illusory—there's no danger here for anyone exercising reasonable care. A steep little start but then the going is easy and the return along the valley a delight.

Shorter Alternatives: (1) The walk can be cut short at almost any point and a descent made to Borrowdale, though this is not advisable in the region of Mabbin Crag, where the ground is steep and rocky. Afforestation may in time make descent to Borrowdale very difficult. (2) the walk up Ashstead Fell and return via Borrowdale is worthwhile and scarcely takes 2hrs gentle strolling.

Bad Weather Alternatives: Visit historic Kendal and see: (1) Abbot Hall Museum of Lakeland Life and Industry; (2) Abbot Hall Art Gallery; (3) Kendal Museum; (4) Kendal Church; (5) Brewery Arts Centre; (6) Castle ruins. Perhaps best of all is to wander the town itself, exploring the various nooks and crannies. Special treat—tea and cakes in Farrer's olde worlde tea and coffee shop!

An Almost Unknown Valley of Great Charm

It isn't generally realised that on the eastern side of the Lake District there is another Borrowdale and another Wasdale. Neither

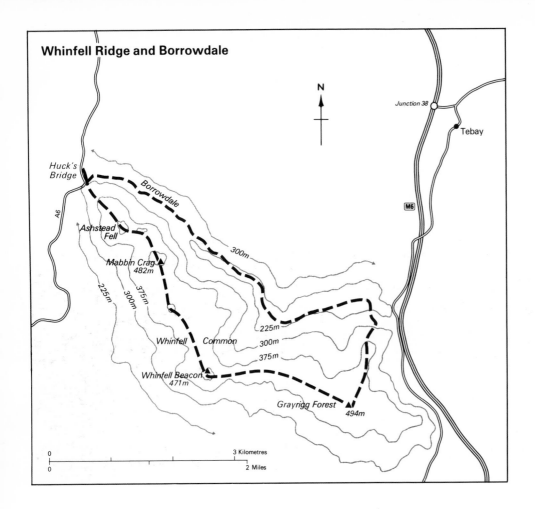

Whinfell Ridge and Borrowdale

N

Junction 38

Tebay

M6

Huck's
Bridge

A6

Borrowdale

300m

Ashstead
Fell

Mabbin Crag
482m

225m 300m 375m

225m

Whinfell   Common

300m

375m

Whinfell Beacon
471m

Grayrigg Forest
494m

0   3 Kilometres

0   2 Miles

valley is as famous as its counterpart further west, although a century or more ago the hotel at Shap Wells, which lies hidden in a fold of the hills at the end of Wasdale, had a reputation as a spa.

The Borrow Beck, which forms Borrowdale, begins life in the undistinguished and little-known fells lying immediately west of the Kendal – Shap road and flows more or less in a straight line south-eastwards until, with a sudden change of heart, it turns almost through a right angle to flow the odd mile or so north-east to join the Lune Gorge. At a place called Huck's Bridge there's a natural gap, north and south, through which the road runs. This cuts off the head of the dale, but it does provide ready access to the rest and especially the splendid Whinfell Ridge which forms the southern side of it.

Since there is also a good road through the Lune Gorge—and a motorway to boot—it does mean that Borrowdale and the Whinfell Ridge are accessible from either end. Parking is not a problem at either place, so one is spoiled

for choice seemingly. My own view is that if you want to stroll along the valley for an hour or two, do so from the Lune Gorge end but if you want to tackle the ridge then the start has to be on the Shap road.

The old road over Shap is the infamous A6, until 1970 crowded with cars and lorries going to and from Scotland, but much quieter since the M6 was built. Lines of heavy vehicles stuck in a blizzard on this road used to be stock winter pictures for television news. In those days vehicles descending towards Kendal would keep an eye out for the Leyland Clock because then they knew the worst was over. The large round clock, topped by the message LEYLAND MOTORS FOR ALL TIME, was a bizarre piece of advertising which stood fifty years by the roadside. It was wound up by a local resident, though it could not always be relied upon to tell the right time! It was supported by a pillar which looked as though it was made from left-over Meccano parts, painted green. The whole thing was moved to the grounds of the Brewery Arts Centre in

Borrowdale and the Howgills from the Whinfell ridge. (Photo: Duncan Unsworth).

Kendal, where it can still be seen. Bearing in mind the problems of Leyland Motors in recent years, the irony of the message is inescapable!

A few yards from where the clock stood a gate gives access to Ashstead Fell, the first peak of the Whinfell Range. Borrowdale, broad and beckoning, lies on the left with a bridle path leading the eye in, but our way too is attractive—up the fellside, not too steep or too far and with a definite ridgy feel about it. There are some rocky outcrops, easily avoided, and then the summit—or at least, one of the summits, for Ashstead Fell has three, would you believe. This one's got the cairn, even though it is the lowest at 1493ft (455m). The others are both 46ft (14m) higher and are soon reached across a little dip.

It's a satisfying sort of fell to climb, which makes it all the more tragic that it is destined to be ruined for the sake of a few trees. Permission has been given to plant conifers on the fellsides and already the drainage work has begun, not only on Ashstead Fell but further

along the ridge too. This will quite ruin the character of these fells and if—God forbid— the reservoir scheme ever goes ahead we could see Borrowdale and the Whinfell Ridge transformed into a pale imitation of Thirlmere. Take a hint: get this walk in now before the developers destroy it!

The path along the summit ridge is quite well trodden which is just as well because the intake walls run right up and over the fells on this side of the valley and the path does indicate where the gates are. It is curious about the walls—on the other side of Borrowdale the intake wall is much lower. I wonder why?

On a fine winter's day, over to the west, the Kentmere fells lie in a great hogsback ridge like a stranded white whale, whilst to the south the sun glistens on the far-off estuary of the Kent. In the north, Cross Fell can be seen like a dusting of icing sugar amongst the clouds and in the east, much nearer than the rest, the lovely Howgills. The snow of winter makes the fells stand out more and in summer only the Howgills would be of any note.

There's a descent and a climb to the next peak on the ridge, Mabbin Crag (1581ft/482m), which takes its name from the series of outcrops lying below the summit on the Borrowdale side. I once tried to descend the ridge at this point and found that the outcrops were decidedly awkward to negotiate and the fellside itself is very steep. This is not the place to come down—much better to go further on, into the broad hollow below Castle Fell, if you want to descend. In bad weather even this might be tricky, but the ridge is very much gentler on its other flank and it is only a matter of minutes to descend to the narrow road along the Ashstead Beck, which leads back to the A6.

Looking down into the narrow Borrowdale valley the romantic white ruins of High Borrowdale Farm can be seen and a little distance away Low Borrowdale farmhouse. This is the only habitation in the valley between the Shap road and the Lune.

The ridge continues over Castle Fell (1568ft/478m) to Whinfell Beacon (1548ft/472m) where there are two tall cairns and extensive views to the south and west. Not only are the principal Lakeland hills discernible (if you can sort them out) but even Whernside and the distant Bowland fells. Much nearer is the British Telecom repeater station, a space-age oddity of struts and dishes, out of place in these fells but symptomatic of what the

authorities can do with a piece of countryside which is not protected by any special status. It is Whinfell's and Borrowdale's misfortune to lie between the devil and the deep blue sea—or rather, between the Lake District National Park and the Dales National Park, not belonging to either. So irrespective of how lovely it might be (and Borrowdale is lovelier than many more famous places in the area) it is open to rape and humiliation: the threat of forestry and of flooding and the planting of electronic gizmos like this one.

Our way actually descends to the British Telecom station before climbing back up again to the final—and highest—summit of the ridge, Grayrigg Forest (1621ft/494m). You can go beyond the summit to the crags known as Great and Little Coum and take an eagle's eye view down into the gorge of the Lune where road, rail and river squeeze together. That funny noise you can hear is not a buzzing in your head caused by altitude, but the distant roar of traffic along the M6.

This gap through the hills caused by the Lune has always been a vital line of communication. The Romans had a road through here, and the line of it can still be seen on the other side of the valley on the lower slopes of the Howgills. They had a fort at Low Borrow Bridge (the site is just the other side of the railway line) and another road ran from there up Borrowdale for three quarters of a mile,

Left: **High Borrowdale Farm from Mabbin Crag.**

Above: **The Borrow Beck has some fine bathing pools.**

climbed up the Whinfell ridge and crossed it where the British Telecom station now stands, then continued to Kendal. Interestingly enough, this road has been resurrected on the southern side by British Telecom to service their equipment, and even on the steeper Borrowdale side it is still a right of way. When the Romans built a road they meant it to last!

From the end of the ridge a descent can be made along the spur known as Birk Knott into the woods which cluster at the end of the valley. Borrowdale Woods look gnarled and ancient like something from a Japanese production of Macbeth. Though the woods are straggly, the individual trees menace.

But the walk through the valley is sheer delight—one of the best valley walks in the Lake District. It would be criminal to flood such beauty under a reservoir.

The road, which is surfaced at first, climbs steadily, passing an old corrugated iron barn which is so decrepit it is becoming an acceptable part of the scene. The fields in this part of the valley look lush and green and in spring are full of fat bouncy lambs. Have you ever noticed how lambs wag their tails furiously when feeding?

A bridge leads the road across a tumbling beck and you might be able to trace the line of the Roman road, because this is where it climbed the fell to cross the ridge. At the gate beyond the bridge the road becomes a rough cart track and leads up the valley (but *down* a slope, curiously enough) to a somewhat worn wooden bridge across the Borrow Beck, the main river of the valley. It's not a bridge I'd like to drive across on a dark stormy night! Just below it though, the stream forms a delectable swimming pool, deep and cool on a hot afternoon.

The views of the Whinfell Ridge are particularly good from this point in the walk: all blues and purples against a declining sun.

The path winds round a corner, past Low and High Borrowdale. The rocky outcrops of Mabbin Crag, tier upon tier of them, are revealed in their complexity and then the path crosses back over the stream by a bridge which has replaced an older one whose abutments can still be seen nearby.

The path stretches ahead through the valley. All that remains is a mile or so of gentle walking.

The Borrow Beck. (Photo: Duncan Unsworth).

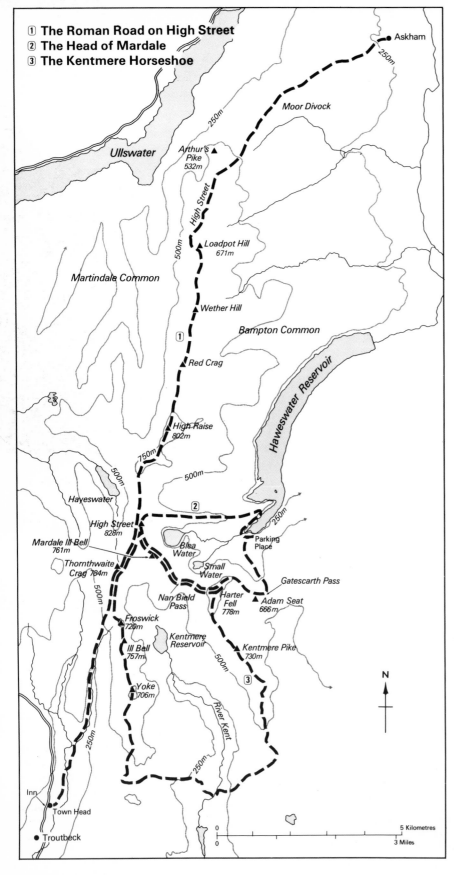

① **The Roman Road on High Street**
② **The Head of Mardale**
③ **The Kentmere Horseshoe**

Askham

Moor Divock

Ullswater

Arthur's Pike
532m

High Street

Loadpot Hill
671m

Martindale Common

Wether Hill

Bampton Common

①

Red Crag

Haweswater Reservoir

High Raise
802m

750m

500m

Hayeswater

High Street
828m

②

Blea Water

Parking Place

Mardale Ill Bell
761m

Small Water

Gatescarth Pass

Thornthwaite Crag 794m

Nan Bield Pass

Harter Fell
778m

Adam Seat
666 m

Froswick
720m

Kentmere Reservoir

Kentmere Pike
730m

Ill Bell
757m

③

Yoke
706m

River Kent

N

Inn

Town Head

Troutbeck

0					5 Kilometres

0   3 Miles

WALK 6: The Kentmere Horseshoe

Above: **Ill Bell and Froswick.**

Map: English Lakes (SE) 1 : 25,000 (A small section of High Street is missing, being on the NE Sheet, but it is not absolutely necessary.)
Start: MR456042. The church at Kentmere village.
Best Approach: Leave the A591, Kendal–Windermere road, at Staveley and follow a narrow road up the valley. A new car park is planned for the village.
Distance: 12 miles (23km).
Time: 7hrs.
What's it Like?: A good introduction to the harder sort of walk; long, elegant, about 3600ft (1100m) of ascent but no big strenuous slopes. Steepest bit is from Nan Bield to top of Harter Fell, after which it seems downhill all the way! There is danger in mist because there are plenty of crags to fall over and under such conditions navigation is not easy between Froswick and Harter Fell.
Links with Other Walks: The route connects with walks **7, 8, 39.**

Shorter Alternatives: By using the Nan Bield Pass it is possible to break the walk into two unequal halves. The western half is longer and tougher than the eastern: say 5hrs against 4hrs.
Bad Weather Alternative: Kendal has many attractions; don't miss Abbot Hall Museum.

A Popular Valley-Head Walk

The vale of Kentmere, along with the neighbouring Longsleddale, is relatively unknown to the average Lake District visitor, who usually goes tearing past, firm in the belief that the Lakes start at Windermere and not before. But the fellwalkers know their secrets, especially Kentmere, where the ring of fells round the valley head has long been one of the classic walks of the district. Though it is fairly long—12 miles—and involves over 3500ft (1050m) of ascent, it is not particularly tough as these things go; less so than the Mosedale or

Coledale Horseshoes, with which it compares. It is an excellent introduction to the harder sort of fell walk.

The walk starts in the village of Kentmere, situated where the valley narrows, almost at the end of the surfaced road. It isn't the valley head by any means—there's another three miles or so—but it seems like the limits of civilization; a pretty place of scattered houses, a church and an ancient pele tower. It is usual to park by the church, which is about the only place there is and even that is limited. There is a plan to make a car park hereabouts soon, so by the time you read this it may have happened.

From the church the route begins steeply up the road to the end of the houses where a sign points to a bridleway, Garburn Pass. This was once part of a major drove road from the west coast to Yorkshire and it was also known as the 'assize road' because jurors from this part of Westmorland would travel along it to the assizes in the county town of Appleby. It is still

broad and quite good underfoot, though back in 1730 the Troutbeck magistrate, Benjamin Browne, ordered the road to be repaired because 'it is not passable . . . without danger of being bogged in the moss or lamed among the stones'. From it there is an excellent view of Kentmere Hall: a fine fourteenth-century pele tower and sixteenth-century statesman's house.

At the top of the pass there's a gate and a wall leading along the crest of a broad ridge, going north. By following this you eventually come to a stile over the wall and a good track which leads to the first of the three distinctive summits making up the ridge proper, Yoke (2316ft/706m). This is quickly followed by Ill Bell (2484ft/757m) and Froswick (2362ft/720m). These three mountains are almost always done together: a regular trinity like the Eiger, Mönch and Jungfrau above Grindelwald in Switzerland, though very much more modest, of course! The main path actually by-passes the tops, so you have to be careful to

The head of Kentmere from Stile End. The Kentmere Horseshoe follows the skyline from left to right. (Photo: Duncan Unsworth).

On the Ill Bell ridge looking towards High Street. (Photo: Duncan Unsworth).

include them if the weather is misty. The path can be boggy, especially near the Garburn Pass. There's a good view of Windermere from Yoke and at the other end of the ridge Froswick gives a sighting of the great cairn on Thornthwaite Crag, the next objective.

Strictly speaking, neither Thornthwaite Crag nor High Street are on the line of march, but it seems a pity to miss them out seeing that they are so near, and most walkers include them. However, if time presses, there is a perfectly good track which contours round the head of Hall Cove to Mardale Ill Bell, the peak at the very head of Kentmere—and not to be confused with *the* Ill Bell which you've just crossed. Ill Bell does actually look bell-shaped when seen end-on along the ridge, more than can be said for its Mardale namesake.

Meanwhile, back at the ridge, the main path is heading for High Street, but in clear weather Thornthwaite Crag's tall cairn is easily seen and the path to it followed over swelling moorland (2572ft/784m).

And what a cairn it is! Anyone accustomed to the usual pile of stones or austere trig block will be both delighted and enchanted by Thornthwaite's 14ft high confection, built in drystone fashion like one of those eighteenth-century chimneys which graced old lead-mining areas. It stands at a corner of a wall, on top of a low crag, and it can be seen for miles.

The view from the summit is nothing much to write home about and the way ahead looks pretty dismal too; a broad cream-coloured track sweeping up a grassy moor to the top of High Street. But as it progresses there are good views of Hayeswater lying in the hollow below and out towards the distant fells above Patterdale. The path by-passes the summit of High Street by quite a way so the thing to do is to follow it until it breasts a distinct rise and all the peaks to the north are suddenly revealed. If you turn right at this point you will cross a grassy sward directly to the trig block, which can't be seen until the last moment (2717ft/828m).

High Street is a small plateau. There's not much to be seen from the trig block, but by walking east a short distance you come to the precipitous east face of the mountain, with awe-inspiring views down to Blea Water and across to Harter Fell.

The walking gathers interest again. Either by following the edge of the corrie south, or by going back to the trig point and following a broken wall, eventually a path is found that leads over Mardale Ill Bell (2496ft/761m) and down to the gap which is the Nan Bield Pass. The views on both sides are quite splendid. To the north is the rugged east face of High Street, Blea Water, Small Water and Haweswater and to the south the vale of Kentmere and the ridge which formed the earlier part of the walk. The Nan Bield itself was once a major pack-horse route linking Kentmere with Mardale, and a direct way from Kendal to Penrith.

The path down from Nan Bield to Kentmere can be used to shorten the walk, though not by much. Scenically, it might even be the preferred route, but of course, it is not the Kentmere Horseshoe. To complete the horseshoe it is necessary to climb out of the gap that is Nan Bield to the summit of the next mountain, Harter Fell (2553ft/778m). The summit of this fell is marked by a cairn comprising tangled metal railings like some mad, *avant-garde* sculpture. It might indeed *be* some modern sculpture for all anyone knows, for who can tell such things with certainty? I am sure the Tate would purchase it, given half a chance.

If you can tear your eyes away from the sculpture, there's a very good view of Haweswater to the north and across to High Street, too. On the south side a broad ridge leads away on the final leg of the journey to Kentmere Pike (2395ft/730m) and Shipman Knotts (1926ft/587m). The route follows a fence and a wall without let or hindrance, grassy at first but rockier at the final peak. Eventually it comes down onto the old bridleway joining Kentmere with Sadgill in Longsleddale, and across this there's a path leading over a grassy moor known as the Green Quarter back to the village.

It's a grand walk and you are probably too tired to wonder why Kentmere has only the Green Quarter, Crag Quarter and Hallow Bank Quarter. Where's the missing quarter?

The old packhorse road in Kentmere along which the final return is made to the village.

WALK 7: The Head of Mardale

Above: **Haweswater from Harter Fell.**

Map: English Lakes (NE) 1:25,000.
Start: MR469108. The car park at the head of Mardale.
Best Access: From the A6 at the north end of Shap village take the minor road to Bampton Grange and Bampton. Turn left at Bampton and follow the signs for Haweswater. The road ends at the car park.
Distance: 6 miles (10km).
Time: 4hrs.
What's it Like?: This compact fell walk encompasses three mountains—Harter Fell, Mardale Ill Bell and High Street—yet is never more than a mile from the car park! Nevertheless it is high and rugged. The path is good throughout, but there are lots of crags around and in mist these could be a danger to the inexperienced, especially between Nan Bield and the top of Long Stile. A compass is useful in such conditions, if only to make sure you are following the right path. In winter this walk—especially the descent—is for experienced and well-equipped walkers only. There is about 2000ft (600m) of ascent involved; not particularly strenuous.
Shorter Alternative: From the Nan Bield Pass descend by a good track past Small Water directly to the starting point. About 2hrs; a very fine short walk.
Bad Weather Alternatives: Visit Askham and Lowther. Askham Hall (not open to the public) is the Elizabethan home of the Earl of Lonsdale and the village is attractive. Lowther Castle is the huge shell of the 1811 Gothic monstrosity in which the family formerly lived. Very impressive. The sporting 5th Earl founded the Lonsdale Belt for boxing and as first president of the Automobile Association gave it the family colours—yellow. Impressive family tombs at MR518245. There is also an adventure park.

Over Harter Fell, Mardale III Bell and High Street

On the eastern edge of the high fells lies the long and lonely Mardale, which in 1937 was flooded to make Haweswater reservoir. There are few people now who remember the valley as it was with the Dun Bull pub, the old school of 1711, the ancient church and Measand Hall, but it was by all accounts a magic place, a sort of Lakeland Brigadoon—or so those who fondly reminisce would have us believe. Perhaps it was; certainly there was something magical about it in the long dry summer of 1984 when Haweswater dwindled to a fraction of its normal size and the ruins of the village emerged from the depths. Thousands of visitors flocked to see the drowned village, to poke in the ruins of the Dun Bull and the church and to cross the perfectly preserved bridge which is usually 30ft (10m) beneath the waves!

So high and imminent is the mountain wall round the head of Mardale that it used to be said the sun never penetrated from Martinmas to Candlemas. Particularly impressive is the craggy face of Harter Fell—not to be confused with the other Harter Fell over in Eskdale which is an equally fine mountain, though quite different from this one.

When they flooded the valley they built an access road along the south-east shore which ends in a car park, often full on a summer's weekend, though there's usually space somewhere. From it the climbing starts straight away—that's one of the nice things about this walk, there's absolutely no preamble and at the end of the day you come down off the fell and you are back at the car within minutes.

The obvious track climbing the hillside from the car park divides within a few yards and the path to the left, less worn than the other, climbs gently up towards Gatescarth Pass, once a major pack-horse route into Longsleddale. The ascent is surprisingly gentle and there is plenty of time for backward looks at the unfolding panorama of the lake. Patches of bog can be irritating, especially just at the point before the summit of the pass where the track slopes off right to climb the fell proper, but the continued ease of ascent is an unlooked-for bonus on a fell which appears so ferocious from below. Before long a cairn appears on a bald grassy top, decorated with a tangle of old iron spars: the remains of the previous fence. It has all the appearance of being the top but it isn't—there's another space-age cairn a few yards further and a few feet higher. This is Harter Fell (2553ft/778m).

The views are quite remarkably distant, embracing all of southern Lakeland and beyond. The Kent estuary and Arnside Knott are prominent and so too are the Pennines. Closer to hand is the distinct ridge of Yoke, Ill Bell and Froswick, looking like a camel with three humps and part of the Kentmere Horseshoe (see Walk 6), as indeed is Harter Fell itself. To the immediate east lie Haweswater, Small Water and Blea Tarn with Mardale Ill Bell (not to be confused with its namesake just mentioned) and High Street as broad massifs bearing, unfortunately, the distinct scar of a well-worn path. On the skyline too, it is possible to pick out the tall cairn on Thornthwaite Crag.

From the summit of Harter Fell the descent to Nan Bield Pass is a delight: narrow and rocky. The pass is a major route from Mardale to Kentmere, and a superb walk in its own right. There are lovely views down into Kentmere and along that valley to Rainsbor-

Haweswater in winter. (Photo: Duncan Unsworth).

From Gatescarth easy slopes lead up to the top of Harter Fell.

row Crag on Yoke—any climber will tell you that Rainsborrow Crag is a bit of a Yoke!

The climb from the pass over Mardale Ill Bell to the summit of High Street is just a steady pull up to a grassy plateau where there is a long drystone wall, now mostly derelict, which should be followed to a concrete trig block (2717ft/828m). One thing to bear in mind on High Street is that the main path across the top, the Roman road, which is temptingly broad, does *not* go to the trig point. Should you find yourself following this highway then the moment the last rise is breasted and the Straits of Riggindale come into view, turn sharp right over the unmarked turf and you will fetch up exactly at the trig block.

From the summit it is a short walk across the almost level top to the east to look down dizzying heights into Blea Water tarn and appreciate the profile of Long Stile and Rough Crag, which is to be the way down. The ridge lies on the far side of the tarn, separating it

from lonely Riggindale; a narrow ridge, straight as an arrow, pointing into the head of Mardale. The way in which it leads directly to the top of the fell is reminiscent of Hall's Fell on Blencathra (see Walk 31), though this ridge is much longer, if not quite as exciting.

There is a small cairn marking the place where the ridge abuts against the escarpment. The path plunges straight down and the ridge, called Long Stile at this point, is at its narrowest. Soon, however, it levels out to a grassy area called Caspel Gate where there is usually a small tarn and where it is possible to descend towards Blea Water and pick up a track which leads back to the car park in a very direct manner. Most walkers, however, prefer to stick with the ridge over Rough Crag until a good path descends towards the lake and joins the shoreline path back to the car park.

The descent of the Long Stile ridge is undoubtedly the climax; a suitable ending to a very fine walk.

WALK 8: The Roman Road on High Street

Map: English Lakes (NE and SE) 1:25,000.
Start: MR507235 The west end of Askham village street.
Distance: 16 miles (26km).
Time: 7hrs.
What's it Like?: A long gentle ascent to High Street and a steep descent to Troutbeck. This descent should not be underestimated, for though the goal is in sight, there are still 4 miles (6km) to go! Good navigation is required in mist because the paths are many and varied, especially round Moor Divock and High Street, and the ridges confusing.
Links with other routes: This walk connects with walks 6, 7 and 8. The walk could be ended by reversing the first part of Walk 6, but descending to Troutbeck. It is more in keeping with the rest of the walk, but not traditional.
Shorter Alternative: An ingenious compromise to overcome transport difficulties, is to start at Pooley Bridge, go as far as High Street, then reverse the first part of Walk 8 to Patter-

dale and catch the boat back to Pooley Bridge. A bit shorter but more arduous. Needs good timing and doesn't complete the Roman road.
Bad Weather Alternatives: (1) Lowther Park—see the church and mausoleum (MR518245) the ruined façade of the castle, the villages of Newtown and Lowther (the latter designed by the Adams') and the adventure park; (2) Dalemain Hall, (3) Penrith.

Walking in the Footsteps of the Roman Legions

Most visitors to the Lake District discover sooner or later that the curiously named fell of High Street is so called because there is a Roman Road across the top of it. In recent years to follow this road has become an increasingly popular pastime with fellwalkers, although it has the disadvantage of being both long and linear, so it is not easy to get back to

Above: **On High Street looking back along the Roman Road which has followed the skyline, on the right.** (Photo: Duncan Unsworth).

the start once the walk is over. A non-participating driver is essential.

In broad terms the route follows the ridge which runs from north to south along the east side of Ullswater, over High Street fell, then down to Troutbeck. A thirteenth-century document refers to the road as Brethstrett, 'the paved way of the Britons', but there is no evidence that the road was used before Roman times. As to the latter, there is evidence in plenty. You can actually see it quite clearly in places—two ditches and a central raised bit—as for example where it starts to climb up Barton Fell from Moor Divock. Archaeologists have also cut sections through it and near Loadpot Hill a section revealed a top layer of gravel, cambered to the edges, then a layer of peat and a final 2ft-thick base layer of rough quarried stone. In general the road shows up light green against the darker moorland and where it has been worn by boots, as on High Street fell, it seems to be standing the strain pretty well.

It is usually assumed that the road ran from the fort at Brocavum (Brougham) to that at Galava (Ambleside) and both the Ordnance Survey and guidebook writers indicate quite clearly the route it took. In fact, the only *certain* line is from the Cockpit on Moor Divock to the start of the Ill Bell ridge. North and south of these points tradition says that the road ran to Tirril and down Scot Rake to Troutbeck respectively, but this is only conjecture. There is some evidence that the road might have gone north-east, towards Askham, and it is more than likely that it kept to the high ground along the Ill Bell ridge in the south.

This means that though the major part of this walk is fixed by the Roman road, the start and finish can be tailored to suit the individual. Most people prefer to walk the route from north to south, starting at Pooley Bridge, ending at Troutbeck. I propose to follow this plan, but starting at Askham instead, because it has always seemed more logical to me, and anyway the quiet dignity of Askham is more in keeping with such a historic walk than the riotous tourism of Pooley Bridge!

From the crossroads in Askham a road leads west through the attractive village to the edge of the moor, where there is good parking. The

Bottom left: **Ancient stone circle at Moor Divock.**

Bottom right: **The Roman Road follows a broad ridge towards High Street.**

road continues but gradually deteriorates as it climbs steadily to Riggingleys Top, where there is a fine copse of trees in the corner of a limestone wall. The paths are a bit confusing at this point but by going straight ahead you meet a signpost marking a curious crossroads of tracks in the middle of a large flat area.

This is Moor Divock, a place of ancient tumuli scattered across a broad saddle. The place is laced with paths but at the crossroads the way ahead is barred by a truly nasty bog and it is better to follow the broad track towards Pooley Bridge until at a large cairn a better path can be found to the Cockpit, a stone circle whose age is unknown. The path from Pooley Bridge joins here and then the route starts to climb the long easy slopes to Loadpot Hill. Once again, the paths can be confusing and it is not unknown for walkers to follow the most obvious path too far—it should be left after crossing Elder Beck—and finding themselves on the way to Howtown. A good sign that this has happened is the deep gash of the Aik Beck which this path crosses. If this should happen to you, then turn left after the beck, climb Arthur's Pike and rejoin the route from there.

Arthur's Pike is a minor peaklet on the flanks of Loadpot Hill, quite craggy on its northern side facing Ullswater, but scarcely discernible from our side. It is worth a visit though, for the extensive views it offers of the lake, the northern fells and the distant Pennines. It is only a few minutes out of our way and in any case, something is needed to relieve the tedium of Loadpot Hill. It must be the most boring hill in the entire Lake District; great swelling breasts of heather and coarse grass, unrelieved by form, content or colour. No wonder they call it a *hill*—the ultimate disparagement in this land of *fells*. The ascent is gentle but inordinately long and the top is adorned with a trig block (2201ft/671m).

The Roman road actually passes to the west of the summit and it is a curious fact that it avoids *all* the summits, though sometimes by the merest of margins. I suppose the Romans had little thought for such niceties, being simply interested in getting from one place to another with the minimum of effort. Incidentally, the track along the Ill Bell ridge misses the summits of Froswick, Ill Bell and Yoke in a similar manner (see Walk 6), which is another reason for supposing it was part of the Roman road.

The route descends to a broad col where once there stood a shooting lodge belonging to the Lowthers then climbs Wether Hill (even less distinguished than Loadpot Hill) and continues along a gathering ridge, over Red

Below left: **The path across Moor Divock looking towards Loadpot Hill, the start of the High Street.**

Below right: **The Ill Bell ridge with (left to right) Froswick, Ill Bell and Yoke. In the foreground is The Tongue and the traditional way to Troutbeck follows a path between The Tongue and the ridge.**

Moor Divock can be reached by a broad path from Pooley Bridge.

Crag to High Raise (2631ft/802m), the second highest summit of the far eastern fells after High Street. The scenery has by this time become quite wild. The deep silent valley of Rampsgill lies on the right while the fells roll down to Haweswater on the left. This sense of high, lonely, places increases as the route reaches Rampsgill Head (2598ft/792m). All around are deep corries edged with lines of shattered crags.

The path descends to the narrowest part of the whole ridge, the Straits of Riggingdale, where on the one hand you can look down into wild Riggingdale as it plunges into Haweswater and on the other into the deep corrie wherein lies Hayeswater. If there are trailers of mist drifting over the ridges there are few places in Lakeland more dramatic than this.

Our route meets a wall at this point and begins the traverse over High Street, a small elevated plateau. As usual, the path misses the summit (2717ft/828m) which is marked by a trig block against the wall. It can be found by turning left just before the path begins its long descent to Thornthwaite Crag. It is worth the diversion, too, to the eastern edge of the plateau, to look down on Blea Water—perhaps the most perfect of high mountain tarns.

This top part of High Street is known as Racecourse Hill. In the old days the shepherds from the surrounding dales would meet here to exchange lost sheep and the occasion became something of a sports' day, with wrestling, jumping and horse racing. It was discontinued about the beginning of the nineteenth century, when the shepherds' meets were transferred to the Dun Bull at Mardale and the Kirkstone Inn.

The main path sweeps down off High Street to the prominent cairn on Thornthwaite Crag (see Walk 6), but this fell is not actually on the line of the Roman road proper, which, as usual, avoids it. Instead, it descends to the start of the Ill Bell ridge, whose camel's humps are most distinctive from here, then descends a very steep path known as Scot Rake into the Troutbeck valley. For the first mile the steepness is quite excessive—leg muscles ache at the strain—but then the angle eases and the walk passes pleasantly through a narrow valley bounded on the one hand by Ill Bell and on the other by a delightful little fell called the Tongue.

Beyond Hagg Bridge lies a farm road known as Ing Lane and this leads towards the final goal, Troutbeck. But it seems never to end and cruelly, after all those miles, it is uphill! The nice surprise is that it ends at a welcome pub, the Queen's Head.

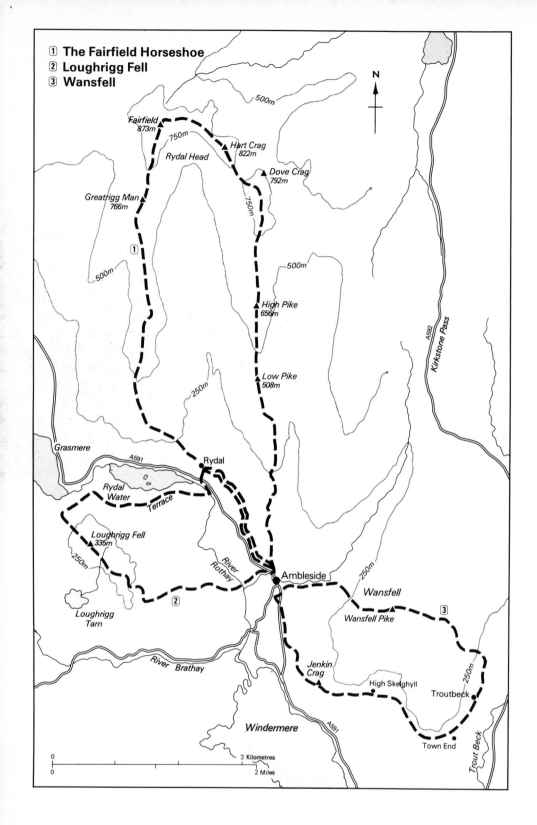

① **The Fairfield Horseshoe**
② **Loughrigg Fell**
③ **Wansfell**

N

500m

Fairfield
873m

750m

Hart Crag
822m

Rydal Head

Dove Crag
792m

Greatrigg Man
766m

750m

① 500m

500m

High Pike
656m

250m

Low Pike
508m

Grasmere

A591

Rydal

Rydal
Water

Terrace

Loughrigg Fell
335m

250m

River
Rothay

Ambleside

② Wansfell

Wansfell Pike

③

250m

Loughrigg
Tarn

Jenkin
Crag

River Brathay

High Skelghyll

Troutbeck

250m

Windermere

A591

Town End

Trout Beck

Kirkstone Pass

A592

0   3 Kilometres
0   2 Miles

WALK 9: Wansfell

Above: **The summit ridge of Wansfell.** (Photo: Duncan Unsworth).

Map: English Lakes (SE) 1: 25,000.
Start: From Ambleside bus station (MR376045) go across the road to the Salutation Hotel and round behind the Sally Bar.
Distance: 6 miles (10km).
Time: 3hrs (not including Town End).
What's it Like?: Good paths throughout and absolutely no technical difficulty, but the ascent of Wansfell is very steep. Stock Ghyll and Town End are well worth seeing and the views from Wansfell and Jenkin's Crag are stupendous.
Shorter Alternatives: (1) Stock Ghyll and back. 1hr; (2) Jenkin's Crag and back. 1^1/2hrs; (3) from the top of Wansfell Pike descend as before but just before Nanny Lane turn right and eventually pick up another lane, Hundreds Road, which joins Robin Lane about half a mile before High Skelghyll. Misses out Troutbeck. Saves half an hour or so.
Bad Weather Alternatives: There are sundry delights in Ambleside including a wide variety of shops, the garden centre, Brockhole National Park Centre (MR390010), and pleasure steamers on the lake.

Ambleside and Troutbeck through Magnificent Scenery

The one building by which Ambleside is instantly recognizable is Bridge House; a tiny house which occupies its own bridge over Stock Ghyll in the centre of the town. It is now owned by the National Trust, but the story that it was originally built by a Scotsman who wished to avoid paying land tax is a local leg-pull for the benefit of tourists! It was actually built as a garden house for Ambleside Hall, probably in the late seventeenth century.

Few people pay much attention to the Ghyll the House stands over and yet it played an

important part in the town's life in former times. It powered various mills and it was one of the prime attractions for the Victorian tourist since half a mile out of town there is the splendid Stockghyll Force. So popular did this waterfall become that some people became very sniffy about it, regarding it as a vulgar tourist attraction (the same sort of people who regard themselves as travellers and everyone else as tourists). They were reprimanded by the formidable Miss Harriet Martineau in her splendid guidebook of 1855:

'It is the fashion to speak lightly of this waterfall—it is being within half a mile of the inn, and so easily reached; but it is, in our opinion, a very remarkable fall (from the symmetry of its parts) and one of the most graceful that can be seen.'

Quite right too, Miss Martineau!

Stock Ghyll and its waterfall form the start to this fascinating walk; one of the best round Ambleside. It begins by following the road behind the Salutation Hotel (signposted to the Force and Wansfell) which soon reaches the ghyll and climbs pretty steeply along its side. At a small housing development (Stockghyll Court, would you believe?) a path slopes off down to the stream which it crosses by a footbridge. There is a choice here, because

paths run along both banks, but I prefer to cross over and follow the true right bank.

The ghyll is now in a gorge, the water difficult to see because of the trees, which grow luxuriantly in the sheltered chasm. There are various paths, but it isn't difficult to pick the right ones (when in doubt go for the ones with the iron guard rails!) and eventually you come to a good viewing point for the cascade which leaps in two bounds a depth of some 80ft. Higher up a bridge spans the stream above the falls and by crossing this and descending a few feet on the other side there are a couple of other good places from which to see the water. It is worth the extra bit of effort because the view is more comprehensive from here.

Through the woods on the right (looking upstream) there's a path leading to a curious iron turnstile gate, like the sort they used to favour for open-air swimming pools; seven feet high and on its last legs I should think. It is probably a relic of the days when there was a charge of 3d to see the falls. It gives access to a tarmac road and by following this uphill for a short way you come to an iron ladder stile bearing the legend, 'Troutbeck via Wansfell'.

Actually, the last few minutes have had an element of sadism about them because Wansfell has been in full view and looking awfully

Above left: **Stock Ghyll Force is the highlight of a short walk up the gill from Ambleside and an interesting approach to Wansfell.**

Above right: **A party of walkers descending Wansfell towards Ambleside. In the background is the High Pike ridge of the Fairfield Horseshoe.**

Jenkin Crag and Windermere.
(Photo: Duncan Unsworth).

which forms part of the Kentmere Horseshoe.

On the Troutbeck side the way down is not nearly as steep as the way up. A pleasant path wanders down until it joins a fell road, Nanny Lane, which is at first green then rocky, but bounded always by its drystone walls, as it descends to Troutbeck, joining the village road a short distance above the Mortal Man inn.

Troutbeck is a long straggling village with more than a score of buildings from the seventeenth and eighteenth centuries, including Town End, now in the care of the National Trust. Our route turns south along the road, through the central part of the village, until at the Institute a lane veers off uphill, signposted to High Skelghyll and Jenkin's Crag. This is the way we want unless—and I strongly recommend it—you have time for a diversion to Town End, a Cumbrian statesman's house *par excellence*. The house is reached by following the road a little further and then, very conveniently, after the visit you can continue in the same direction and take a lane which brings you back to the original line.

This is known as Robin Lane and is not unlike the earlier Nanny Lane, though not as steep or rough. It winds round the hill, all the time giving superb views of Windermere. In earlier times it formed part of the same pack-horse trail as the well-known Garburn Road from Troutbeck to Kentmere. After a while a tarmac road comes up the hill to meet the lane and leads on to the farm at High Skelghyll. Beyond the farmyard it becomes a track again, plunging into the Skelghyll Woods.

After a few minutes a National Trust notice on the left announces Jenkin's Crag and a short path, looking a bit like a badly made patio in suburbia, leads towards an obvious viewpoint. Like Stock Ghyll, Jenkin's Crag was one of the great Victorian 'sights' without which no visit to Ambleside was complete and as is so often the case, the Victorians knew a thing or two. The view of Windermere is superb; like the view up Borrowdale from Friar's Crag on Derwent Water (a contemporary viewpoint), this is one of the great views of the Lake District.

Beyond Jenkin's Crag the bridleway crosses a little bridge then, getting rougher underfoot for a while, zigzags down until it once more becomes a sedate lane. It ends with a bird's eye view of Hayes' Garden Centre, recently equipped with Ambleside's version of the Crystal Palace, or perhaps it is Xanadu . . .

Follow the town's Old Road back to the car, or the pub.

steep. You can usually comfort yourself with the thought that few mountains are ever as steep as they look. Unfortunately, Wansfell is.

The path is on turf and not well defined at first although the way is obvious. It climbs to another ladder stile, then steepens and remains steep right to the very top. Not for Wansfell that nice slackening off you get near the top of many fells; if anything, this one gets steeper and the last few feet are positively little rocky craglets through which the path zigzags. The top (1588ft/484m) is marked by a few stones.

The point is actually called Wansfell Pike and curiously enough, it is not the highest point on the Wansfell Ridge. There is one at the other end of the ridge, about a mile away, which is ten feet higher, but only purists go there for it's an awfully boring place.

The one good thing about the steep ascent is the justification it gives to stop and admire the view. And it is worth admiring. There are aerial views of the town and beyond the town the distant mountains march across the skyline from Coniston to the central fells and beyond. From the summit the view expands to include the length of Windermere as well as Rydal Water, Grasmere, Elterwater and sundry tarns. The Kent estuary glimmers on the southern horizon and beyond it are the distant Bowland Fells and the unmistakable profile of Ingleborough. Kirkstone Pass shows prominently on the eastern horizon, Red Screes, Thornthwaite with its great beacon, and the Ill Bell ridge

WALK 10: Loughrigg Fell

Map: English Lakes (SE) 1:25,000.
Start: Ambleside car park, on left of main road at north end of village. (MR375047)
Distance: 6 miles (10km).
Time: 3hrs.
What's it Like?: A very varied walk. Despite its lack of height, Loughrigg is a rough old fell. Confusing in mist. About 1000ft (300m) of climbing and a bit of a grind at first, but nothing excessive. The Terrace views, over Grasmere, are justly famous.
Bad Weather Alternatives: (1) Take a trip on a lake steamer to Bowness or Lakeside; (2) Hayes Garden Centre—extensive both inside and out; (3) Brockhole National Park Centre (390010)—fine gardens, well laid out exhibitions, famous teas.

An Autumn Wonderland

Ambleside is to the southern Lake District what Keswick is to the north: the heart of tourism. It dominates the central valley and from it one can easily reach Langdale, Patterdale, Coniston, Kentmere and—less easily perhaps in view of the narrowness of the Hardknott and Wrynose passes—Dunnerdale and Eskdale. Someone once called it 'the axle at the wheel of beauty', a fanciful reference to Wordsworth's original concept of the Lakeland valleys being like the spokes of a wheel.

Certainly at the time of the Lake Poets Ambleside and Grasmere were regarded as the heart of things and this continued more or less throughout the Victorian period. Industrialists from Lancashire and Yorkshire built their mansions here, and the good and famous came for holidays, including Charlotte Brontë, George Eliot, Waldo Emerson, John Bright, Humphrey Davy and Dr Arnold of Rugby. There were no large estates as in other parts of Britain, but nevertheless the offcomers planted

Above: **Loughrigg is one of the finest viewpoints in the Lakes. Looking north-west one sees the Langdale Pikes and Easedale fells, with Grasmere in the foreground.**

Above right: **On Loughrigg Terrace**.

Above left: **The Eastern Fells seen from Loughrigg**.

many trees, including maple and copper beech, which along with hazel coppice and other local woodland helped to transform this part of the Lakes into a golden wonderland in late autumn.

Loughrigg Fell is Ambleside's own personal mountain. It rises on the doorstep, so to speak, and so can hardly be ignored. It can be surprisingly confusing in mist, but it's a grand little walk in good weather—including a clear winter's day—with some very fine views.

The start is not very prepossessing. Just beyond the car park, along the main road, the first road off to the left is marked 'cul-de-sac', but despite this there is a footpath at the end of the road which wanders across the fields to Miller Bridge over the Rothay, where it meets a surfaced lane near a T-junction. One branch of the lane climbs steeply up the hill and though it is signposted 'private road', it is a right of way for pedestrians. In hot weather these initial few feet of climbing are quite tiring, which is an excellent excuse for pausing to look at the view back over Ambleside and the eastern fells.

After half a mile or so the road becomes a bridleway and leads up to the old clubhouse of the defunct golf course. Golf on Loughrigg must be akin to cricket on the Goodwin Sands,

and it is small wonder the club closed down some thirty years ago due to lack of support! The clubhouse is now a private residence.

At this point the bridleway becomes a path and climbs up into the hummocky ground of the fell tops. The hummocks are small outcrops of rock which were smoothed off by glacial action in the times when all this area was covered by ice. In between the hummocks the hollows are peat filled, sometimes with tiny reed-fringed tarns. This distinctive landscape can be seen elsewhere in the district and is known to geographers as mamillated topography. I leave you to guess why.

A little tarn is passed where you gain a first glimpse of Langdale and then the path climbs steadily until a large cairn comes into view. This isn't on the path, but it is worth the short diversion because it gives a superb vantage point for Langdale, Loughrigg Tarn and the Coniston Fells. The Langdale Pikes look specially magnificent from here, and it is probably true to say that the view is better than from the summit itself.

From the cairn the path descends a little before rising again to the trig block on the summit of the fell (1099ft, 1355m).

The view from the summit is not as attractive perhaps as the previous one, but it is

51

certainly widespread. With the exception of the northern fells, where only Skiddaw shows, almost every group of fells in the district can be seen. The topography of the Lakes is laid out like a scale model. It is a worthwhile exercise to stand with Wainwright's *Central Fells* in your hand identifying all the peaks and lakes from the detailed diagrams he gives of the views from Loughrigg. There is no better way of fixing the various features in their proper context and so getting to know the layout of the district.

There was a time when the way down to Loughrigg Terrace from the summit was a steep runnel where the path had been eroded away by weather and a million boots. It really *was* steep, and perhaps tricky if you weren't a seasoned fellwalker, but at least it was natural. It was replaced by an abominable flight of steps which would look out of place in a municipal park, never mind a national park.

This is our way, unfortunately. Down the steps to the Terrace, which is a level path curving round the fell.

Loughrigg Terrace is one of the most famous short walks in the Lake District and it is easy to see why. It is convenient to the road and centres of tourism, it is short and without fatigue, but above all it gives an absolutely stunning view over Grasmere to Helm Crag. There's an island in the lake and attractive woods all about, and in autumn especially the scene is quite breathtaking. There are golds and browns and greens in glorious profusion.

By following the Terrace to the right, around the corner of the fell, Rydal Water comes into view. It is smaller than Grasmere but quite jewel-like in its setting. Were there ever another two lakes in England to match this pair?

At this point a little care is needed in selection of the route for it is easy to follow the main path which goes too low for our purpose. A smaller, but still distinct, track rises round the fellside and leads to an enormous cave. It is possible to go in at the entrance along a bit of a gangway, but otherwise the cave mouth is filled with water—a vast, Stygian, underground lake. Lower down the fellside there is another, smaller cave: both are the abandoned remains of slate quarrying.

The path now descends rapidly to the River Rothay at Pelter Bridge. In autumn the trees here are truly magnificent and together with the old arched stone bridge form a colourful and memorable picture.

It is possible from here to follow the narrow motor road by the Rothay, along the foot of

Helm Crag and Grasmere seen from Loughrigg Terrace. (Photo: Duncan Unsworth).

the fell, back to our starting point. It passes a number of dwellings with literary associations, including Fox How, built by Dr Arnold as a holiday home in 1833 where his son, Matthew Arnold and grand-daughter Mrs. Humphry Ward visited. A more interesting option, however, is to cross Pelter Bridge and walk up the road to the narrow lane which leads to Rydal Hall.

Rydal is where Wordsworth spent the last 37 years of his life. His best work was already done, at Dove Cottage in Grasmere, but it was to Rydal he came to enjoy the rewards of his labours. It was here the man of letters became the living legend.

He helped to place the church at the end of the lane near the road in 1824 and he gave his daughter a field behind it now known as Dora's Field, where masses of daffodils bloom in the spring. (On her marriage Dora lived at Loughrigg Holme, the fourth building on the right along the Loughrigg road from Pelter Bridge.) Wordsworth himself lived at Rydal Mount, the building at the end of the lane which can be visited during the summer months. On the other side of the lane is Rydal Hall, home of the Flemings for many years, but now a conference and study centre for the Diocese of Carlisle.

A bridle-path can be followed which leads through Rydal Park, starting at the Hall, and joining the main road again at Scandale Bridge, from where it is only a few minutes' walk to the car.

WALK 11: The Fairfield Horseshoe

Above: **Grasmere from Heron Pike.**
(Photo: Duncan Unsworth).

Map: English Lakes 1:25,000. Both the SE and NE maps are required.
Start: MR 376047. Ambleside car park.
Distance: 10¹/₂ miles (17km).
Time: 6hrs.
What's it Like?: A bold sweep around the Rydal Beck; a high-stepping ridge which in fine weather has no intrinsic difficulties. In poor visibility great care is needed between Fairfield and Dove Crag where there are many crags on the eastern side. Can be done in reverse, but one misses the long ridge descent into Ambleside.
Shorter Alternatives: (1) See Walk 9, Wansfell and Walk 10, Loughrigg Fell; (2) Reverse the route described from the car park to Low Sweden Bridge over the Scandale Beck. Continue as if to climb Low Pike for rather less than a mile then, at a sheep-fold, turn right and cross the beck again by the delightful High Sweden Bridge. From here there is a path parallel with the stream, back to Ambleside. About 3 miles

(5km) in all; allow a couple of hours' gentle amble.
Bad Weather Alternatives: Ambleside has all sorts of goodies, from the National Park centre at Brockhole (MR390010), to pleasure steamers on the lake. If the weather lifts for an hour or so, go and see Stock Ghyll (see Walk 9).

A Famous High Circuit of the Rydal Fells

Rydal Beck penetrates deep into the heart of the Fairfield massif and in so doing forms two long ridges, one on either flank, which link together round the head of the valley to form a classic horseshoe. It is the most readily accessible of all the great horseshoe ridge walks because it can be done on foot from Ambleside without any travelling to remote dales. Moreover, it encompasses no fewer than eight

53

distinct peaks, seven of which are over 2000ft (600m).

By its very nature a horseshoe walk starts in one place and finishes in another, so something has to be done about linking the ends. In this case it is very easy because the ends are little more than a mile apart; a level mile through Rydal Park, which is best taken at the start of the day. Leave the car in the car park at Ambleside and walk along the main road to Scandale Bridge, beyond which is a pair of large gates and a signpost to Rydal Hall: the start of the broad track through the park to Rydal.

In these fields the Rydal Sheepdog Trials are held each August. The way through them leads to the massive hall, once the home of the powerful Fleming family and now a diocesan centre for Carlisle. Between the hall itself and the outbuildings the way continues until it meets the hamlet of Rydal.

Apart from the hall, Rydal is just a small collection of church and cottages in a cul-de-sac off the main Ambleside–Keswick road. At the top end of this little lane is a rather more substantial house, Rydal Mount, which is where William Wordsworth spent his last years full of honours and fame. House and gardens are kept much as they were in the poet's time and they are open to the public.

Not that there is time to visit Rydal Mount on this walk! Instead, the way goes past the house along a walled lane which ultimately becomes a rather steep repaired path zig-zagging up to the open fellside. The path climbs steadily up Nab Scar until it reaches the ridge line, then it follows the ridge to Heron Pike, the first real summit of the walk (2008ft/612m).

It is worth pausing here to admire the string of lakes in the valley below, stretching from Grasmere to Windermere like pendant jewels. Up ahead the ridge sweeps away like a roller-coaster towards the flat-topped Fairfield. On our own fell, Erne Crag juts out to cut off the view of the head of Rydal Beck, but enough can be seen of this shallow vale to mark it out as uninviting—especially in winter when it can look particularly bleak.

A broad path leads to Rydal Fell (2037ft/ 621m) and then Great Rigg (2513ft/766m) before climbing up to the top of Fairfield (2864ft/873m).

Fairfield has a considerable plateau for its summit and the best views can only be got by walking round the rim so as to have uninterrupted vision. Even so, the mighty panoramas which embrace most (but not quite all) of the Lake District are impressive only by magnitude—'Never mind the quality, feel the width!' Except in winter when the snow transforms every view into an alpine wonderland, views like that from Fairfield tend to be, well, boring. I fully appreciate that this is

Far left: **Rydal Mount was once the home of William Wordsworth.**

Left: **The pretty hamlet of Rydal where the ascent begins.**

likely to be regarded as curmudgeonly at best, heretical at worst, but I am increasingly of the opinion that the most aesthetic views are from quite lowly fells like Loughrigg or Wansfell. I claim no originality for this—Ruskin was of the same opinion, of course.

So far there has been little danger attached to the walk but between Fairfield and the next summit, Hart Crag, huge cliffs fall away from the ridge on the eastern side. It is worth leaving the established path to take peeks over the edge into Deepdale and Link Cove, though care is required. In misty conditions this part of the ridge can be very tricky.

Once the beehive-shaped summit of Hart Crag (2697ft/822m) is reached, the safety factor is increased by a remarkable drystone wall which begins just beyond the peak and continues along the crest of the ridge all the way down to Ambleside. In bad weather, of course, all one needs to do is follow the wall, keeping to its left hand side. This is what the path does in any case.

The wall leads first to Dove Crag (2598ft/792m) which is an innocuous summit taking its name from the savage-looking cliff on the eastern side which forms such a splendid head wall to Dovedale. Then the ridge (and the wall) turn south and head for home.

At first the ridge is broad and grassy as it reaches High Pike (2152ft/656m) then narrower and littered with attractive rock outcrops as it descends to Low Pike (1667ft/508m). It is surprisingly long for a lateral ridge—over a mile and a half—and the two summits give it an air of quiet distinction. From below it looks most attractive.

Beyond Low Pike there's a choice of route. Either cross Scandale Beck by the ancient and romantic-looking High Sweden Bridge or stay on the same side and cross it much lower down by the Low Sweden Bridge. Either way is a fine walk and both lead directly to Ambleside and the car park.

The High Pike ridge seen from Loughrigg. The last part of the horseshoe follows the ridge from left to right.

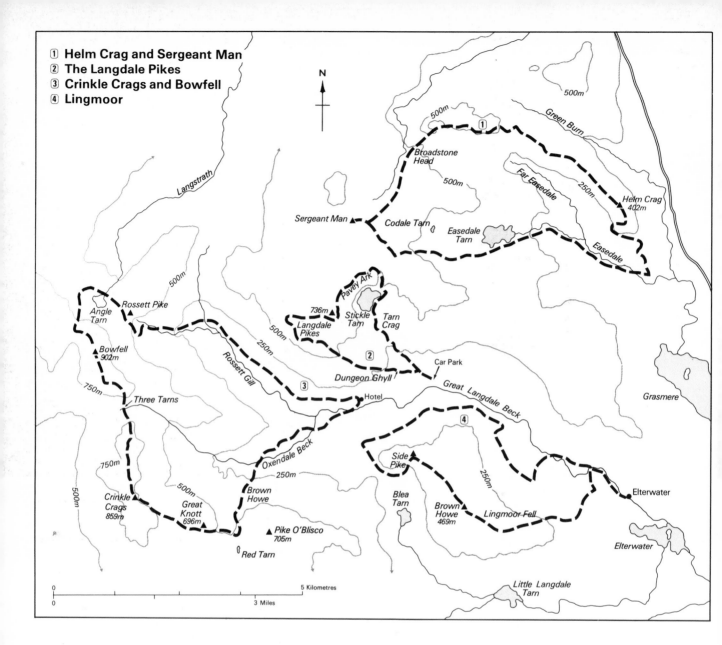

1 **Helm Crag and Sergeant Man**
2 **The Langdale Pikes**
3 **Crinkle Crags and Bowfell**
4 **Lingmoor**

N

Langstrath

500m

500m

Green Burn

① 500m

Broadstone
Head

500m

Far Easedale

250m

Helm Crag
402m

Sergeant Man ▲

Codale Tarn

Easedale
Tarn

Easedale

Angle
Tarn

Rossett Pike ▲

500m

Pavey Ark

736m

Langdale
Pikes

Stickle
Tarn

Tarn
Crag

250m

▲ Bowfell
902m

500m

Rossett Gill

②

Car Park

750m

Three Tarns

③

Dungeon Ghyll

Hotel

Great Langdale Beck

Grasmere

750m

Oxendale Beck

250m

④

500m

Crinkle ▲
Crags
859m

500m

Great
Knott
696m

Brown
Howe

Side
Pike ▲

250m

Blea
Tarn

Brown
Howe
469m

Lingmoor Fell

Elterwater

▲ Pike O'Blisco
705m

Red Tarn

Elterwater

Little Langdale
Tarn

0
0

5 Kilometres

3 Miles

WALK 12: Helm Crag and Sergeant Man

Above: **Lonely Codale Tarn (left) and Easedale Tarn (right) mark the way down.**

Map: English Lakes (SW and SE) 1:25,000. This walk lies at the corner of all four sheets of the Outdoor Leisure Map. The two mentioned will suffice and you could get by with the SW sheet alone, which only omits the village.

Start: MR335080. A car park on the Easedale road out of Grasmere.

Distance: 8 miles (13km). Circular.

Time: 5hrs.

What's it Like?: A splendid introduction to the high fells; not long, but quite serious. Good navigation required in bad weather, when the trip is suitable only for experienced fellwalkers. Sergeant Man is almost the centre of the Lake District fells.

Shorter Alternatives: (1) Climb Helm Crag and return same way—1¹/₂hrs; (2) walk up Easedale to the tarn and return same way—1¹/₂hrs; (3) from Moor Moss return via Far Easedale—4hrs.

Bad Weather Alternatives: Dove Cottage and the Wordsworth Museum. The home of the Wordsworth industry! Just off the A591 at Town End. (MR 342070).

The very Heart of The Lake District

Grasmere village, nestling in a bowl of the fells at the foot of Dunmail Raise, is for many people what the Lake District is all about. It has a lake, or mere, from which it takes its name, attractive white cottages, a good pub and a stunning setting. Each August there is the rush-bearing ceremony for the church and later in the month the famous Grasmere Sports with fell-racing, hound trailing, Cumberland and Westmorland style wrestling and other events. Above all it has Wordsworth. The poet lived at Dove Cottage from 1799 to 1808, then

57

at the Rectory and Allan Bank and finally at Rydal Mount from 1813 until his death in 1850. He is buried in the churchyard.

Towering over the village is the shapely Helm Crag (1306ft/398m), with two groups of rocks on top which have been given fanciful names like 'the Lion and the Lamb' and 'the Old Woman Playing the Organ'. There is a point on the Dunmail Raise road where the former name makes sense, but the Old Woman can only be seen to proper effect from the Easedale track—and even then, you have to look hard. A good viewpoint for Helm Crag is Loughrigg Terrace: the classic view of the fell and the lake (See Walk 10).

Helm Crag is a popular walk in its own right, easily done from the village in a morning and back to the Red Lion in time for a lunch-time pint. So too is the other end of our walk, Easedale and up to the tarn, with the picturesque waterfalls of Sour Milk Gill on the way. This too can be done in a morning's stroll. The link between the two, however, over the curiously named Sergeant Man (which is a mountain, not a person) is as remote a walk as you are likely to find in these pages.

A narrow road leads out of the village towards Easedale and just before Goody Bridge there is a car park on the right which could hardly be more convenient. Further along the road meets a narrow footbridge where the Easedale track veers off whilst the road itself continues across an open field which looks like parkland to a cluster of old houses and a parting of the ways. A signpost points to Helm Crag and the route goes up a rocky alleyway to eventually emerge on the fellside near a flimsy barrier and a notice telling all and sundry that the way to the top has been changed because of erosion.

Human erosion is a problem affecting paths in all our national parks. The sheer weight of numbers means extraordinary wear on the surface, especially where it is something soft like easily eroded peat as it is in parts of the Pennines. In the Lakes the erosion wears away the clay and gravel of the paths and leaves the large knobbly rocks which are difficult to walk on, causing visitors to abandon the proper path for the edges, which wear away in their turn. The result is a broad scar across the landscape. Improvements can only come about if the paths are given time to recover, if nature is allowed to reassert itself. In the meantime, however, the pressure of tourism carries on relentlessly and some compromise has to be found. Unlike more remote parts of the world, which have similar problems—the Nanda Devi

The desolation of Brownrigg Moss near the head of Far Easedale, with the Eastern Fells beyond. (Photo: Duncan Unsworth).

sanctuary in the Himalayas, for example—we cannot close the national parks to tourists, nor even, as the Americans do, restrict entry to a limited number. Our national parks are not wilderness areas; they are created by man and man still lives and works there.

The usual way out of the dilemma is simply to improve the paths. This can be done in a variety of ways, some more sympathetic to the environment than others. In the case of Helm Crag, however, an entirely new path has been constructed—and very well done it is too.

The old path, shown on the maps, was fairly steep. It climbed the crest of the fell between the east and west faces and in descent offered aerial views of Grasmere, village and lake. The new path starts steeply, past some old slate tippings, but soon levels off to traverse magnificently across the west face of the fell with superb views over Easedale and the fells beyond. Eventually it swings back east to join forces with the old path, just a little distance below the top.

A summit ridge 250 yards long runs south-east to north-west along the top of the fell. At each end are groups of rocks, pointing skywards aggressively like Stone Age missiles. I am not prepared to enter into the argument as to which is the actual highest point. The

Above: **The Gibson Knott ridge from Helm Crag. The walk follows the ridge, then left across the head of Far Easedale.** (Photo: Duncan Unsworth).

Below: **The Old Westmorland-Cumberland boundary fence at the head of Far Easedale.** (Photo: Duncan Unsworth).

Ordnance Survey say it is the south-east rocks, almost everyone else says it is the other rocks and some long-gone fellwalker, probably a senior civil servant, has constructed a conciliatory cairn between the two!

The popular names given to these rocks mean nothing at close quarters. The south-east summit (the official Lion and Lamb) is an easy scramble, if a bit airy, but the north-west summit is distinctly harder to reach, needing a few simple rock-climbing moves. Not counting isolated pinnacles like Pillar Rock or Napes Needle, little Helm Crag probably has the most technically difficult summit in the Lakes!

The Helvellyn ridge lies spread across the eastern skyline, with Seat Sandal and Fairfield. The path up Tongue Gill to Grisedale Hause can be traced quite distinctly even at this distance and peeping over a shoulder of Fairfield is Cofa Pike and St Sunday Crag. Away to the south the view is much more pastoral, with the vale of Grasmere and Windermere, woods and water and the hummocky fell of Loughrigg. North the view is restricted by Steel Fell and the western skyline is the unexciting ridge of High Raise and the long barren vale of Far Easedale leading up towards Greenup Edge.

Beyond the north-west summit of Helm Crag the ridge dips then rises to the next high point, Gibson Knott (1379ft/420m). The path is small but well formed and more or less follows the crest the whole way. It is an attractive walk, with lots of little rocky outcrops to enliven the scene and compensate for the fact that the path starts to get boggy beyond Gibson Knott. The ridge rises to Calf Crag (1762ft/537m) but the path misses the top and sweeps down to the great bowl of Moor Moss, which is the head of Far Easedale.

What a desolate scene this is ! Far Easedale, rocky, barren, with a gurgling beck and a sombre crag called Deer Bield, full of difficult rock climbs and, sweeping round from the north-east, the upper wastes of the Greenburn valley, surely one of the boggiest places in the Lake District.

The desolation is emphasised by the tattered remnants of a wire fence erected years ago, which once marked the boundary between Westmorland and Cumberland, in the good old days when counties were properly constituted. You passed from one county to the other by means of an iron ladder stile, which still exists, standing uselessly in the wasteland like something out of a painting by Dali.

The main path here is not the one we are following but one at right angles to it, climbing out of Far Easedale to cross the moor and Greenup Edge *en route* for Stonethwaite and Borrowdale. As a youngster I travelled this way quite often, usually from the youth hostel at Rosthwaite to one in Grasmere, or vice versa, on wartime jaunts guided by an enthusiastic schoolmaster whom we called Jasper, though his real name was Harry. It was a walk none of us ever tired of; a magnificent way of walking from one valley to the next.

Our way, however, lies up the craggy-looking fellside to the south-west. The tatterdemalion fence now comes into its own because the path is a bit tenuous and the fence posts act as guides. They go exactly the way we want to go. There's not many of them and you'll have a hard time following them in a mist. On the right, the deeply set Mere Beck rushes down towards Wythburn and by turning round to look north you can see Skiddaw and Bassenthwaite Lake. Codale Head comes suddenly, and you find yourself looking across a sprinkling of tarns at the curious cone of Sergeant Man (2414ft/736m).

What a strange mountain this is, both in name and aspect. It can be climbed from the surrounding moor in a matter of minutes and it turns out to be nothing but a rocky pimple—a summit which is nothing but a

summit, a mountain without a body! The real mountain is High Raise, but who climbs a boring fell like High Raise? The best view is over to the south where there is the rear side of Pavey Ark and Harrison Stickle and beyond them the Coniston Fells.

This view improves as we follow the ridge along towards Blea Rigg. An astonishing panorama includes the Langdales, Stickle Tarn, Side Pike and all the fells beyond. The path goes down to a junction where the way comes over from Stickle Tarn to Easedale and it is followed down to Easedale Tarn; a steep, rough walk with views out over lonely Codale Tarn, perched on a ledge with the grander tarn of Easedale below it.

At the tarn the walking becomes easier. There was once a refreshment hut at the point where Sour Milk Gill issues from the tarn. Did I once buy lemonade here during the war? I have that impression, though it might well be memory playing tricks. The hut existed until fairly recently as a steadily decaying ruin, until it was pulled down and the site tidied.

The reason for the hut's existence becomes apparent within the next few minutes. It stood at the climactic point of one of the district's most popular strolls in Victorian days—from Grasmere to Easedale by the rushing waters of Sour Milk Gill and ending with the *coup d'oeil* of Easedale Tarn, reached after a final steep pull. The placing of the refreshment hut was a masterpiece of psychology!

The walk to the tarn is still popular today, mainly because Sour Milk Gill is such a splendid sight when in spate—a pell-mell rushing, pouring, awesome waterslide. Incidentally, there are two other Sour Milk Gills in the Lake District: one in Buttermere and the other draining Gillercomb near the head of Borrowdale. The latter is also a splendid sight in spate.

It is from near here that some semblance of an old woman playing the organ can be seen in the rocks at the north-west summit of Helm Crag. Grasmere lies ahead, near and tempting now, just a gentle stroll along the valley to the car.

Two walkers approach Sergeant Man by the Blea Rigg ridge. In the background, the Langdale peaks.

WALK 13: Lingmoor

Above: **Lingmoor Tarn with the Pikes in the background. The great gullies of Pavey Ark stand out clearly.** (Photo: Duncan Unsworth).

Map: English Lakes (SW) 1:25,000.
Start: MR328047. Car park near Elterwater bridge.
Distance: 7 miles (11km).
Time: 3 hrs.
What's it Like?: A fairly steep climb to the ridge, on good paths, but very easy thereafter. Good views. Excellent exercise for active grannies.
Shorter Alternatives: (1) By using the Langdale bus between Elterwater and the Old Dungeon Ghyll Hotel the walk can be halved. Over the summit to the Old Dungeon Ghyll, about 2hrs. Walk along valley, about 1hr. (2) there is a very fine walk by Elter Water to Skelwith Bridge (a section of the Cumbria Way), about 1hr, return by bus.
Bad Weather Alternatives: (1) Visit the timeshare village (328049)—good restaurant for the affluent, excellent pub grub for us of more modest means—entrance on the main road; (2)

see what can be done with slate at Kirkstone Greenslate display rooms, Skelwith Bridge—Café and gift shop (not just slate!). (345034)

A Quiet Walk on the Langdale Fells

Lingmoor is the mass of hummocky fells dividing Little and Great Langdales. It can be well seen from the road as you approach Elterwater: low and undistinguished, wooded in part and scarred by quarry workings. At its far end—above Old Dungeon Ghyll—it manifests itself more forcibly as a curious little spiky summit called Side Pike, beyond which is Blea Tarn and the low farmhouse, huddled against the fellside, which was the home of Wordsworth's Solitary.

The place could hardly be described as

popular. There are too many counter-attractions to set against it: the Langdale Pikes, Bowfell, Crinkle Crags—heady company for a small fell like Lingmoor. Yet it offers a simple walk with some very fine views of these other mountains, illustrating yet again Ruskin's theory that the best vantage point is from a mountain of modest height. Certainly Lingmoor is modest—1539ft (469m); the neighbouring Bowfell is nearly twice that.

The walk starts in the village of Elterwater, a cluster of cottages nestling at the foot of the fell, and the site of a controversial timeshare complex which occupies the site of the old gunpowder works. The main criticism seems to be over the size of the development, but the place is beautifully designed and well screened by trees and is infinitely preferable to what was there before. In the centre of the village is the Britannia Inn, one of Lakeland's best-known hostelries and beyond it is the bridge over Great Langdale Beck where this walk commences.

The way lies first alongside the beck on the far side from the pub, then the path climbs and goes through quarry workings as it rises steadily through the woods towards the ridge. It breaks free from the trees to reach a quite distinct ridge line. Here the path turns sharply right to follow a wall along the ridge. There is a curious hollow on the left and numerous quarries large and small lie scattered about the moor, for the fine green slate is amongst the best there is and has been worked for many years. Surprisingly perhaps, slate quarrying is still the largest employer of male labour in the Lakes.

It is not far to the summit. The views are extensive in every direction and, like Lough-rigg, this fell is excellent for getting to know the layout of the Lakeland peaks. The view north, to the Langdale Pikes, is especially outstanding and is the best view of these popular mountains you are likely to see, for each can be separately identified—which is not always the case because they are rather bunched together like bananas. The great half-moon crag of Pavey Ark is very impressive.

By leaving the shelter of the wall and heading north from the summit cairn the small Lingmoor Tarn is met with, which provides an admirable foreground for the crags of the Pikes across the valley. From the tarn a path goes back towards Side Pike, crosses the wall, and runs below the rocky peak to the metalled road leading to Little Langdale. Side Pike is quite invulnerable from this angle and indeed the only way up—unless you are a rock-climber—is by the west ridge, following a wall from the road.

There is no need to follow the tarmac road down to Old Dungeon Ghyll, thank goodness, for it tends to be a steep racetrack with bad bends where nervous drivers crash their gears and sometimes their cars, mainly because they have insufficient faith in their machine or themselves. After descending it for a few yards there is a very distinctive left bend where a path runs off directly down to the National Trust camp site.

From the camp site a valley path goes to Side House, then below Oak Howe Crags to Oak Howe and down to the riverside which it follows to New Bridge. Across the bridge, by keeping between the beck and the main road, the latter can be avoided until another footbridge leads you back across the stream to join the very path you set out along earlier.

Descending Lingmoor, with Side Pike to the left and the Langdale Pikes beyond. (Photo: Duncan Unsworth).

WALK 14: Crinkle Crags and Bowfell

Above: **A winter's day: Upper Eskdale seen from Bowfell. Harter Fell is the prominent pointed peak left of centre.** (Photo: Duncan Unsworth).

Map: English Lakes (SW) 1:25,000.
Start: MR286061, Old Dungeon Ghyll car park.
Distance: 9 miles (14km).
Time: 5 hrs.
What's it Like?: This is one of the most popular ridges in Lakeland and rightly so. Delightfully rocky, littered with outcrops which are either easy scrambles or can be avoided. The Bad Step isn't all that bad; just a couple of committing moves on large, polished holds and no exposure. The return from Angle Tarn often takes walkers unawares—it seems very long at the end of the day.
Shorter Alternatives: (1) The route can be split into two walks by means of the Band; Crinkle Crags, descending by the Band, about 6 miles (10km); up the Band and over Bowfell, returning via Rossett Gill, about 7½ miles (12km); (2) start as for Crinkle Crags but at Browney Gill continue to Red Tarn, then turn left and climb Pike o' Blisco; short and sharp, 4 miles (6km).

Bad Weather Alternatives: (1) Visit the Kirkstone Greenslate Gallery at Skelwith Bridge—craft shop and café (345034): (2) retreat to the multiple delights of Ambleside.

A Famous Walk Around the Head of Langdale

The fells which ring the head of Langdale are amongst the best known in the Lake District. The two principal ones are Crinkle Crags and Bowfell, which respectively form the head walls of Oxendale and Mickleden, the two branches into which Langdale divides. Separating these branches of the dale is the long, high tongue of land known as the Band, which points like a spearhead down the valley.

The fells look remarkably rocky, and so they are, though there is only one place, called the Bad Step, which needs pause for thought and that nobbut just, as the locals might say. On

the whole these are high-stepping ridges of the traditional sort.

The walk starts in the car park of the Old Dungeon Ghyll Hotel (also the terminus of the Langdale bus service) and follows a broad lane through the field to Stool End Farm. The way through the farmyard is signposted, but within a short distance the track for the Band veers off uphill and we follow the path into Oxendale–a sombre vale, if ever there was one.

The path leads to a memorial bridge across the Oxendale Beck. Great, lumpy Pike o' Blisco rises ponderously overhead and the track we want climbs by the side of this just before a distinctive ridge known as Markeens. The ascent is very steep. In its upper reaches it looks down into the impressive ravine of Browney Gill and the angle eases somewhat as Red Tarn is approached. Just before the tarn a conspicuous track curves off towards the Crinkles ridge and this is the way we must follow, fairly steeply at first, but more gradually as the ridge is attained.

The ridge stretches ahead as a series of rocky beehives, with the great cone of Bowfell brooding in the background. There are supposed to be five of these summits (or Crinkles), but I have always found it a little confusing to distinguish between what is and

what isn't a Crinkle. However, the first Crinkle is fairly obvious and quite lengthy—some 350 yards—and it leads to a grassy depression with a formidable-looking rock pile on the far side.

A badly eroded scree slope funnels towards one small part of the rock, a short chimney-like fissure which seems to be the only way up. This is the celebrated Bad Step, claimed by Wainwright to be the hardest part of any regular path in Lakeland. Don't you believe it—Yewbarrow is harder, in my opinion, or the direct summit route of Glaramara. The Bad Step is nothing more than a bit of a thrutch, as climbers would say. I have no intention of telling you how to tackle it, on the basis that if you don't know you shouldn't be there. There are actually ways of avoiding it—but I've no intention of telling you about those, either!

Suffice to say that, flushed with exertion and a few palpitations, the summit cairn of the second Crinkle is reached and it proves to be the highest point on the ridge at 2818ft (859m).

There are no more problems on the rocky ridge. The path ribbons, following differing ways over the various Crinkles and it scarcely matters which you take. Each has its own assortment of rock steps, bog patches, tiny pools and spiky pinnacles. The entire ridge is a maze of rock outcrops.

Above left: **A rescue helicopter hovers below the impressive rock walls of Bowfell Buttress.** (Photo: Duncan Unsworth).

Above: **The first snows of winter powder Crinkle Crags. The bad step is on the rocks at the foot of the depression, left of the highest point.**

The view down Langdale from the Band; the best known way to Bowfell. (Photo: Duncan Unsworth).

These come to an end at a broad saddle of bog known as Three Tarns, presumably on the basis that this is the minimum number to be found there at any time. This is where the path up the Band arrives at the ridge and is thus a major junction because the route up (or down) the Band is one of the most popular in the district.

On the other side of the col lies Bowfell, showing the Links, a curious set of seemingly uniform gullies which once attracted rock-climbers but now seem very much out of favour. The path climbs up to the right of the Links, directly to the summit cairn (2959ft/902m). The view is extensive.

Across the summit of Bowfell the way is uncertain and very rocky. The idea is to follow the ridge round to Ore Gap and from there descend the good track to Angle Tarn. However, in fine weather it is usual for the walker to find himself looking over Hanging

Knotts at the tarn below and scrambling down between the rocks. Whether this is worth the effort when there's a perfectly good path round the corner is another matter, but I can vouch for the fact that *at the time* it seems the right thing to do!

Angle Tarn is a deep, broody place. The path we want climbs up steeply and broadly to the lip of Rossett Gill, then it swings away across the fellside, easing the angle before being dragged back by the gill where it gives a couple of zig zags before proceeding more sedately to the footbridge at the base of Stake Pass.

It's a 2-mile (3km) walk from here back to the Old Dungeon Ghyll Hotel; a rough track, a long track for the end of the day. It leads straight back to the car.

Is this a hard walk? Well, hard enough perhaps. But take heart—I once knew a young man who ran the whole thing *before breakfast!*

WALK 15: The Langdale Pikes

Map: English Lakes (SW) 1:25,000.
Start: MR295065 New Dungeon Ghyll. There are two car parks.
Distance: 4 miles (6km).
Time: 3 hrs.
What's it Like?: A short but interesting traverse amongst some splendidly rocky peaks. Could be tricky in mist because of the many crags, but otherwise not dangerous or strenuous.
Shorter Alternative: Walk up Mill Gill to Stickle Tarn and back the sameway.
Bad Weather Alternatives: The valley diversions include the timeshare development at Elterwater (328049), (note: the sports club etc are only available to members, but there is good grub to be had in the bar and restaurant).
There's the Kirkstone Greenslate display at Skelwith Bridge (345034) and ultimately, the multiple delights of Ambleside.

A Traverse of Langdale's Spectacular Crags

The Langdale Pikes are a group of mountains clustered at the head of Langdale on the north side of the valley. They are compact, rather pointed and very rocky. They are not particularly high and yet they dominate the scene like nothing else; in appearance they are the most striking group of peaks in the entire Lakes. They seem to be visible from everywhere in the southern fells, but this is probably because they are so instantly recognizable. With the Langdale Pikes it is a case of once seen, never forgotten.

And the visual impact of the Langdale Pikes should not be underestimated. Though they are fun to climb, this is one case where the goods really look better in the shop window. Start to play with them and they lose some of their magic. The total concept of the Pikes is

Above: **The Langdale Pikes. In the foreground is the National Trust camp site and in the middle distance is the Old Dungeon Ghyll Hotel. From left to right the peaks are Pike o'Stickle, Loft Crag, Harrison Stickle and Pavey Ark. The route follows the obvious slope above the lower crags.** (Photo: Duncan Unsworth).

Harrison Stickle from Pike of Stickle – the well-marked path proves rather steep. The route from the valley reaches the ridge at the extreme right of the picture then follows the top of the rocks towards the camera. (Photo: Duncan Unsworth).

much more than a sum of their parts . . . the grouping is perfect and you would have to travel a very long way—to the Cuillin of Skye in fact—to see anything as fine.

This being so it is worth considering where some of the best views of the Pikes can be got. Everyone has their favourite viewpoints but here are some of mine: *the Lowwood Hotel on Windermere; the lower summit of Loughrigg; Loughrigg Tarn; Elterwater; Lingmoor Fell; Bowfell; Allen Crags* and in winter, *Tarn Hows.*

Some of these views appear as pictures in this book, associated with various walks.

The walk itself starts from behind the New Dungeon Ghyll Hotel, ignores the Stickle Tarn path which has been repaired with all the subtlety of a Roman road, and turns left through a gate then climbs up past a wooden seat to beyond the intake wall where it crosses Dungeon Ghyll.

There seems to have been a proliferation of 'ghylls' in Lakeland in recent years (the correct word is 'gill') but at least Dungeon Ghyll has tradition on its side. Ever since the days when it was an object of Victorian curiosity

Dungeon Ghyll has been spelt thus. The gill is a deep chasm, full of waterfalls and romance such as our forefathers loved. From the place where the path crosses the gill it is possible, with care, to pick your way upstream to where a 60ft (18m) waterfall is spanned by a natural arch—the very embodiment of the Romantic ideal. You must retreat by the same route though—the rest of the gill is virtually inaccessible to all but hardy scramblers and in its higher reaches it is very difficult.

After crossing the gill the path climbs at a steady angle up the fellside with the gill on the right and more or less out of sight. A diversion can be made to the top of the natural arch and some daring souls have been known to walk across it although it is not to be recommended. Dizzying depths yawn below.

The path is actually following a long natural ramp across the fellside which is only interrupted where the path zig-zags up past some outcrops to reach a sort of small plateau. Thorn Crag is on the right and the higher Loft Crag on the left and the path climbs up between them. (Before the final climb a diversion left can be made to look at Gimmer Crag, which is one of the great traditional rock-climbing areas. But you don't get a proper impression of Gimmer doing this and it is hardly worth the effort.)

Once the crest line is reached the whole magnificent concept of the Langdale Pikes falls to pieces. The thing's a sham; a mere facade. Those magnificent craggy fronts are—well, just fronts—there's no depth to them at all. Behind the Pikes is just a dreary wasteland.

But that doesn't mean we can't explore the Pikes themselves. From the col we can turn left to climb Pike of Stickle, a formidable-looking rock beehive, which proves to be not so tough after all. Generations of walkers have always pronounced it as Pike *o'* Stickle and from the top (2326ft/709m) the other Pikes look quite impressive, with gaunt rock walls plunging into the valley.

The long, steep and eroded gully just east of Pike of Stickle is the site of the well-known 'axe factory'. A band of hard volcanic tuff outcrops here and pieces readily flake into sharp edges when struck. This was discovered by Neolithic man who set up a 'factory' making axe-heads and similar artefacts. It was a fairly sophisticated operation—the axes were sent elsewhere for finishing (it has been suggested they went to gritstone areas for sharpening) and were exported as far as the Continent. The 'factory' was discovered in 1947, since when the gully has got steadily worse due to human erosion and is now positively dangerous. Beware— keep away; all the axe-heads have gone.

Across the bog of Harrison Combe the path strikes boldly up Harrison Stickle, at 2415ft (736m) the highest of the Langdale Pikes. The view extends along Langdale, across Windermere and out to the eastern fells. Nearer to hand is the grand craggy face of Pavey Ark, rising from Stickle Tarn.

Pavey is our next objective and it turns out to be merely a short stroll from Harrison Stickle. The summit is about 2300ft (700m) but nobody bothers with the summit on this fell because it is really just a great big crag which could be regarded as the south-eastern face of Thunacar Knott, an otherwise totally undistinguished mountain. The top of Pavey is knobbly, as though the crag didn't want to stop, and it is very rough rock, reputedly a patch of gabbro, the roughest of the rough.

It is time now to turn for home, and the way down from Pavey Ark lies at the north-east end of the crag where a distinctive grass rake cuts straight down through the rocks. In misty conditions this might be difficult to find in

Above: **Descending Stickle Gill (Mill Gill) in winter. Pavey Ark can just be seen above the lip of the corrie.**

which case by working north a bit, easier ground can be found which leads to Bright Beck and Stickle Tarn. But the rake itself is both unusual and very quick as a means of descent.

It is usually a bit boggy where Bright Beck enters the tarn, but this is the place to get the best view of Pavey Ark. What a grand crag it is! The deep chasms of Little Gully and Great Gully make dark slashes on the left, but the most remarkable feature is the big slanting ledge called Jack's Rake which cuts across the crag diagonally from bottom right to top left. To follow it is the ambition of every active fellwalker, for Jack's Rake probably represents the limit of what a fellwalker might achieve without encroaching on the world of the rock-climber or enthusiastic scrambler.

For most of its way, Jack's Rake is enclosed in a trough which shields the walker from exposure but unfortunately it breaks out into the open just where the crag is highest. On a fine day the narrow ledges are likely to be crowded with all the world and his wife going up and down (climbers use it as a quick descent after climbing on the crag) so you need a fair degree of confidence in steep places if you want to enjoy Jack's Rake.

There is a small dam at the tarn's outflow

Left: **The repaired footpath up Stickle Gill (Mill Gill).**

because the water was once used as a source of power in the valley. When the dam deteriorated about thirty years ago the tarn almost disappeared, so it was restored by the National Park authority. Because of the dam and its uses the beck tumbling down from the tarn to Langdale was always known as Mill Gill, but recently it seems to have been renamed Stickle Gill, or even—according to the Ordnance Survey—Stickle Ghyll. I often wonder who makes these changes, and why . . .

The path by the side of the gill has changed too. Over the years the path (or paths, for there was one on each side of the beck) became increasingly worn until they evolved into textbook examples of human erosion, frequently quoted by environmentalists. Something had to be done and the National Trust took the job in hand, realigning the path entirely. Unfortunately, though the job is a solid piece of work which will last at least a century, it lacks any sensitivity with the environment. But who knows? Time is a great healer, and given ten or twenty years the path by Mill Gill might become naturalised.

One thing is for sure—it makes for a very rapid descent and leads directly to the New Dungeon Ghyll.

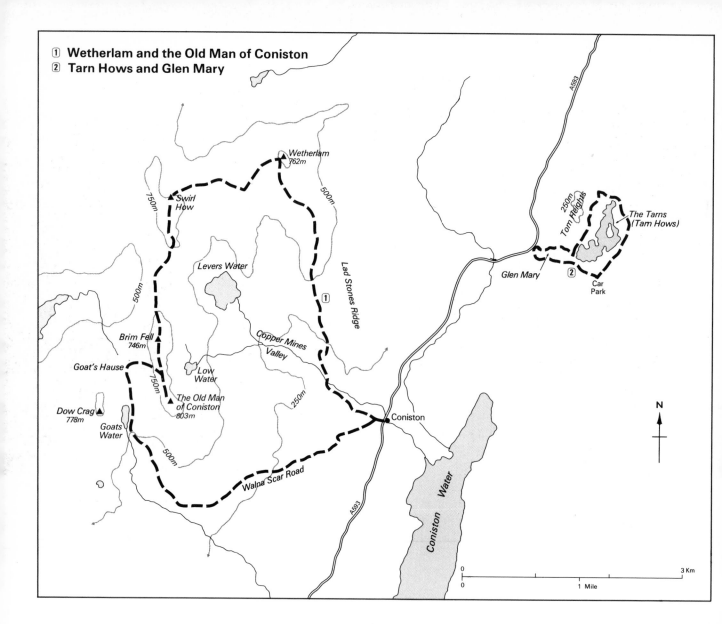

① **Wetherlam and the Old Man of Coniston**
② **Tarn Hows and Glen Mary**

Wetherlam
762m

Swirl
How

750m

500m

Levers Water

①

Lad Stones Ridge

500m

Brim Fell
746m

Goat's Hause

750m

Copper Mines
Valley

Low
Water

The Old Man
of Coniston
803m

250m

Dow Crag
778m

Goats
Water

500m

Walna Scar Road

Coniston

A593

A593

Tom Heights

250m

The Tarns
(Tarn Hows)

Glen Mary

②

Car
Park

Coniston
Water

N

0 ─────────────── 3 Km
0 ─────────────── 1 Mile

WALK 16: Wetherlam and The Old Man of Coniston

Above: **Coniston Old Man (left) and Dow Crag (right) from Swirl How.** (Photo: Duncan Unsworth).

Map: English Lakes (SW). 1:25,000.
Start: MR302976 Coniston car park.
Distance: 7 1/2 miles (12km).
Time: 5hrs.
What's it Like?: A fine, compact ridge walk of the traditional sort. If the weather is good it makes a suitable introduction to the high fells for anyone who has previously just dabbled. Good compass work needed in bad weather, or it could be a long walk home!
Shorter Alternatives: (1) The walk can be left or joined at Swirl Hause by a path from the youth hostel past Levers Water – fascinating country with many mining artefacts; take care! (2) descend from the summit of the Old Man by the direct route as mentioned in the text—saves about an hour; (3) reverse the route described as far as the top of the Old Man then descend the direct route. 6 miles (10km). 4hrs.
Bad Weather Alternatives: (1) Visit Brantwood, Ruskin's home and also the Wainwright museum; (2) go for a sail on the *Gondola,* an original lake steamer resurrected by the National Trust.

Coniston's Finest Ridge Walk

Above the little town of Coniston there rises a shapely group of peaks isolated from the others, forming a little mountain world of their own. Before the redrawing of county boundaries in 1974 these peaks were in Lancashire and the highest of them, Coniston Old Man, was also the highest point of that county. So Lancashire not only lost its slice of Lakeland, it also lost its county top—that honour being transferred to a shapeless lump called Gragareth in the Pennines.

The glaciers have carved out a number of cirques which are particularly well defined in

71

this group of fells and one of them, holding the large tarn of Levers Water, looks down on Coniston itself. The cirques make some wonderful ridges, the best known of which sweeps round Levers Water from Wetherlam to the Old Man making one of the neatest, most compact ridge walks in the Lakes. It is possible to add some outlying peaks like Carrs and Grey Friar to the walk, but doing this spoils the line and few walkers bother.

The walk begins in the car park in Coniston village and goes over the bridge and through the village to where a path starts, behind the Sun Hotel, along Church Beck. At the charming Miners' Bridge the way crosses the beck and joins the small road which has also come up from Coniston. The road leads to the youth hostel and Miners' Row—both remnants of the great copper mining activity which flourished in this valley for several hundred years. There are other industrial remains for the curious to examine and talk of a study centre, but if you do go poking about beware of open shafts and tunnels. (There is a special guide to the remains: *Coniston Copper: A Field Guide* by Eric Holland, which points out what is and is not safe to explore).

However, our present route does not lie up the Coppermines Valley, but follows a path up the fellside just before the row of cottages, to a curious depression called Hole Rake. From here a path climbs steadily and lengthily up the prominent Lad Stones Ridge of Wetherlam. The ridge is a broad whaleback which offers superior views of the surrounding fells. The curious rock of Kennel Crag below Levers Water looks like a broken molar and the two tarns of Levers Water and Low Water are true mountain jewels, the steep fellside shooting up

from their shores. In the rashness of youth I once climbed the Old Man direct from Low Water (there's a perfectly good path only a few feet away) and it is not something I would recommend. It is very, very steep.

On the left of the ridge is the deep valley caused by Red Dell Beck, once the scene of much mining, and despite appearances this too can make an interesting way up Wetherlam as an alternative to the ridge. Indeed, almost every route up this fell is very fine—Black Sails Ridge and Wetherlam Edge are the other principal ones—which is perhaps why Wetherlam has always been a favourite mountain with fellwalkers.

The first part of the Lad Stones never seems to end, but then it changes and soon the large cairn on the top of Wetherlam appears (2500ft/762m). The views are extensive because Wetherlam is singularly isolated, even from the rest of its own group, so there is nothing to interrupt the outward view. Most impressive, though, are the nearer views, especially of Great and Little Carrs: a dark, forbidding crag seamed with deep gullies. There is no rock climbing on Carrs—too rotten for that—but in winter the gullies give good sport and look very impressive when seen from Wetherlam.

Black Sails (2444ft/745m) is a subsidiary summit a few hundred yards south-west of the main summit and can be taken *en route* to Swirl Hause, though the path misses it out, preferring to keep well down the flanks of the fell until it meets the pass. The Hause (which for some obscure reason the Ordnance Survey call 'Hawse') is a dramatic place to be at any time but when the wind shreds the clouds against the Prison Band and shifting light plays on lonely Greenburn and its tarn, it is

The ridge from Swirl How to Coniston Old Man.

The ordinary way down from the Old Man is becoming very worn. Coniston and the lake lie below.

shimmering coast on the other.

Reaching the top of the Old Man brings major decision time. The choice of a way down depends upon the mood of the moment and the time available. The most frequent descent is the obvious one which goes down through the spoil heaps and past the quarry until a path can be taken which joins up with the Church Beck at Miners' Bridge. It is easy and very quick but has nothing else to recommend it especially since it has become badly eroded. Better by far to take a bit longer and retrace your steps towards Brim Fell then slope steeply down the path westwards to Goat's Hause; a distinct saddle between the main ridge and that of Dow Crag.

An eroded path plunges down towards the little tarn called Goat's Water, enfolded in the hollow between the Old Man and Dow Crag. It is a sombre puddle, not the sort of place where the sun smiles often or for long and like Swirl Hause, it can have Wagnerian qualities when the mists shred themselves on the rocks of Dow Crag. The crag itself is immense, probably the largest in Lakeland after Scafell, with great bulging buttresses and deep dark gullies. The climbing has a simple direct quality on Dow, like muscular Christianity, with some hard modern lines added to the old classics.

The path traverses the east shore of the tarn to some distinctive slabs where often there are novice climbers practising their craft, then twists away down the fellside below the old Barrow Climbing Club hut to meet a very broad track known as the Walna Scar Road. In earlier days climbers used to try and get their cars as far as possible up this 'road' to save the long walk to the crag but were always stopped by a unique pair of natural gates which squeezed the road into a ribbon and beyond which no car could possibly get. Even to reach the gates was quite a feat which did no good at all to either springs or exhausts.

The road itself is an ancient green lane used for quarrying and once known as Walney Scar Road. Names do seem to change round here—Goat's Water was originally Gate's Water so it is said, and Dow Crag is pronounced *Doe* Crag, which has led to some confusion in the past.

It is now simply a steady tramp back to Coniston, first along the improving path then at Fell Gate along the modern quarry road which dips steeply down the hill where the old Coniston railway station used to stand and so to the centre of the village and the car.

Wagnerian in concept. Faced with Prison Band as the way ahead—a soaring rock ridge—the innocent walker may well blanch a little, because it looks pretty fearsome, but in fact it is one great big sham. Prison Band is just a delightful rocky romp to the summit of Swirl How (2631ft/802m).

Swirl How is on the main north–south ridge which joins Carrs to the Old Man. It turns out to be remarkably mild-looking considering the dramatic face it shows to Coniston. A great green roly-poly ridge rising and falling on its way to Coniston Old Man. It is easy walking, over Brim Fell (2608ft/796m) and then up to the summit of Coniston Old Man (2635ft/803m) where there is a large slate-built platform like the remains of some misplaced Inca temple. The view is widespread, from the sombre tarns cradled by the ridges, to the distant Scafell peaks on the one hand and the

WALK 17: Tarn Hows and Glen Mary

Map: English Lakes (SE) 1:25,000.
Start: Car park at MR330994.
Best Access: And only access, if it comes to that! Leave the B5285 Hawkshead–Coniston road about a mile out of Hawkshead, at Hawkshead Hill, by a very narrow road on the right. From Coniston there is no need to go all the way to Hawkshead Hill; a slip road joins our route a little earlier. Signposted Tarn Hows. The road is *one way only* and once embarked upon there is no alternative than to go round the circuit, emerging at the bottom of the hill near Monk Coniston. Car park in the woods above the lake, well signposted.
Distance: Negligible—you would be pushed to make it exceed a mile and a half.
Time: Stroll round in an hour.
What's it Like?: Tarn Hows is included in this book because it is just about the most popular beauty spot in the Lakes and justifiably so. It is difficult to include it in a longer walk of any merit, though I have frequently walked over from

Hawkshead by the Keen Ground and enjoyed it—esoteric pleasures. If you want to wander lonely as a cloud, this is not the place to do it. You might find yourself alone at 6 o'clock on a wet Monday morning in March, but I doubt it. Popular with a capital pop. The view is such that it has appeared in just about every sort of pictorial art form, from calenders to hoardings and postcards to television. If you think chocolate-box art isn't real, you obviously haven't seen Tarn Hows.
Bad Weather Alternatives: (1) Explore Hawkshead, a charming village associated with Wordsworth's schooldays—See Anne Tyson's cottage, the old grammar school, the church; (2) Hill Top (370955), in Near Sawrey, the farmhouse home of Mrs Heelis, better known as Beatrix Potter, creator of Peter Rabbit *et al.* Original manuscripts on show. If you think Tarn Hows is popular, you should see this place! Crowds and delays possible. (3) Brantwood (313958), on the east shore of Coniston Water.

Above: **Tarn Hows.** (Photo: Duncan Unsworth).

Tarn Hows from the north. (Photo: Duncan Unsworth).

The home of John Ruskin (1819-1900). A Wainwright Gallery showing original sketches etc, is a recent addition. There is also a Ruskin Museum in Coniston village (Yewdale Road). (4) Grizedale Visitor and Wildlife Centre (336943). Forestry Commission natural history display, nature trails etc. The Theatre in the Forest has evening concerts and lectures. The Centre has recently (1987) had a major facelift.

Lakeland's Most Popular Tarn

Tarn Hows is a little lake lying in the wooded heights between Coniston and Hawkshead and is one of the great honeypot sites of British tourism. The view is romantically beautiful and has been exploited to the full by the media: a few years ago it was plastered over half the billboards in Britain, advertising something or other. Small wonder three quarters of a million tourists a year visit the tarn.

There's perhaps a touch of irony in the fact that this most perfect of Lakeland landscapes is man-made. Until the last century there was a collection of small pools here known as Monk Coniston Tarns, or simply the Tarns, and it

wasn't until a small dam was built across the outflow stream, Tom Gill, that the present attractive sheet of water was created. The Ordnance Survey still call it the Tarns.

The resulting lake was quite shallow, which is one of the reasons it readily freezes over in the winter. Three small islets were left sticking out of the water, the largest planted with trees. Plantations, mostly of pine and larch, were made all about including a couple which reach down to the water's edge, softening the outline of the tarn. Given a century of progress, all this has now harmoniously blended in with the natural scenery.

The tarn is long, narrow and very irregular in shape. The usual view is from the south bank, looking across the water towards the lumpy knolls of Tom Heights, with the superb Langdale Pikes in the background. It is a spectacular piece of landscape at any time of the year, but perhaps at its best in late October when, like so much of southern Lakeland, it blazes with the tints of autumn. Winter too can be quite spectacular and almost Dickensian, with the Langdale Pikes dusted in Christmas

snow and couples skating on the tarn. (Alas, unromantic statistics show that February is a better bet for skaters!)

The property belongs to the National Trust and they have made sterling efforts to try and preserve Tarn Hows against the human erosion caused by millions of boots. Cars are tucked well out of sight and worn areas of grass reseeded. Paths are cared for, too and Tarn Hows is an excellent example of land management on behalf of the people.

Of course, this is not the place to come if it is solitude you are seeking, nor indeed if it is a good hard walk you want. Those things can be found described elsewhere in the book, but this short walk round Tarn Hows should be done by everybody at least once, for it really is strikingly beautiful. I'll let you into a secret, too—once you get a couple of hundred yards from the main car park area, the crowds disappear!

From the car park it is best to do an anti-clockwise circuit of the tarn, keeping along the path at the top of the slope which sweeps down to the water. There is a prominent knoll within a short distance which gives an excellent view of the tarn and the Langdales. Away to the right are the eastern fells, less spectacular than the Pikes in summer, but looking positively alpine under winter snow. The path continues round the tarn through the two woods and breaks out of the Intake Plantation on the slopes of Tom Heights. These rocky hummocks can be climbed for the wider view they offer, but the way then goes down to the shore where the path traverses round to Tom Gill.

The deep little valley carved by Tom Gill is known as Glen Mary. It is scarcely half a mile long, but it is a pretty place, especially in spring with a rather steep path through the woods. It emerges onto the A593, Coniston road, and though there are alternative ways back to the tarn, none can match Glen Mary and the best plan is simply to turn round and climb back the way you came. The car park is only a few minutes' walk away.

Tarn Hows and the Langdale Pikes.

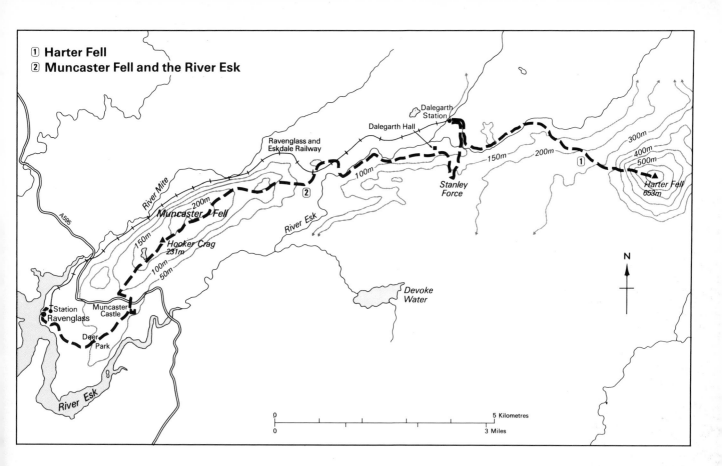

① **Harter Fell**

② **Muncaster Fell and the River Esk**

Dalegarth Station

Dalegarth Hall

Ravenglass and Eskdale Railway

River Mite

A595

Muncaster Fell

200m

150m

100m

50m

Hooker Crag 231m

Station Ravenglass

Muncaster Castle

Deer Park

River Esk

River Esk

100m

150m

200m

150m

Stanley Force

Devoke Water

①

300m

400m

500m

Harter Fell 653m

②

N

0   5 Kilometres

0   3 Miles

WALK 18: Harter Fell

Map: English Lakes (SW) 1:25,000.
Start: MR173007 Car park at Dalegarth Station.
Distance: 7 miles (11km).
Time: 4hrs.
What's it Like?: A gentle stroll along the river bank is followed by a fascinating ascent of the rocky fell. Not recommended in misty conditions, but on a fine day this is a straightforward up-and-down ascent.
Shorter Alternatives: (1) From Penny Hill Farm instead of climbing the fell follow the good path up the valley to the foot of Hardknott Pass, then climb the pass for about a quarter of a mile until it is possible to take a path on the left to Hardknott Roman Fort. Return the same way. About 6 miles (10km) of easy walking, there and back. (2) parking is not easy on the Eskdale road, but there is some space just beyond the cattle grid at the foot of Hardknott Pass. From here a sloping path leads up Harter Fell and joins the route described near Spothow

Gill, Saves about 1½ hrs, but misses the river.
Bad Weather Alternative: As the rain drips down, stand on the parade ground of the Roman Fort at Hardknott, and consider what the Roman squaddies must have thought of such a posting!

River Pools and Rock Outcrops

If ever there was a beauty contest amongst the fells of Lakeland, then Harter Fell in Eskdale would probably win first prize. This is because, though not particularly high, it looks every inch a mountain, with nothing to jar the senses. It is so well proportioned that the very rightness of it strikes a response in every fellwalker's heart immediately.

It is an isolated peak, lying between Eskdale and Dunnerdale, bounded on the north by the notorious Hardknott Pass and on the south by

Above: **Looking out towards the coast from Harter Fell. The dark mass in the foreground is the Green Crag ridge. Devoke Water is in the distance.** (Photo: Duncan Unsworth).

78

Harter Fell from Eskdale. (Photo: Duncan Unsworth).

Station, the Eskdale terminus of the famous 'La'al Ratty' railway. A few yards up the valley from the station a narrow lane leads off the road towards the river, where it meets some stepping stones and the tiny church of St Catherine, once the goal of the Corpse Road over Burnmoor, before Wasdale Head got its own church. There are paths on both banks of the river, though the more intimate views of the various pools are to be had on the north bank. On a hot summer's day the temptation to bathe is almost irresistible and in this respect the Esk is only paralleled by the Langstrath Beck which flows into Borrowdale.

The path leads past the ruins of a former bridge and within a few minutes arrives at the romantic Doctor Bridge where the Esk is crossed and a lane followed to Penny Hill Farm. Through the farmyard another track leads to a divergence of paths, the main one going up the valley to Hard Knott and the other, signposted 'Harter Fell', pointing much more uphill! This is the one we want, following a wall until it crosses a gulch and then the fast-flowing Spothow Gill.

On the other side of the gill the main path leads across the side of the fell to Grassguards and Dunnerdale and it isn't always easy to spot exactly where to turn off for Harter Fell itself. However, should you miss it, follow the main path until the edge of the forest is reached then turn left and climb steadily up the fellside, avoiding the various outcrops.

It is a magnificently rocky fell, though the various crags are not really big enough to attract the attention of climbers. Scramblers can have a grand time of it, however, especially by keeping round to the left of the route of ascent and working their way from outcrop to outcrop. Let me hasten to add that such scrambling is not necessarily easy—some is quite tough and exposed and not for the inexperienced.

The summit proves to be a triple one, three quite separate blocks of which the centre one is just the highest at 2142ft (653m). The summits require a bit of scrambling too! From the top the best view is of upper Eskdale and the Scafell group, though clever-dicks like to see if they can recognize the *other* Harter Fell, way over in the east. It is visible.

The return, of course, is along the route of ascent, though you can walk back along the other bank of the river if the mood is on you. If the river is high, however, be warned—the stepping stones might be under water, in which case continue to the next bridge which fortunately is not far beyond the car park.

Ulpha Fell and Birker Moor. A narrow motor road crosses the latter and from it there is a lovely view of Harter Fell, with the pinnacled ridge of Green Crag in the foreground. Unfortunately, the Duddon face of the fell is spoilt by Forestry Commission plantings, but this is more than made up for by the superb aspect it presents to Eskdale. This is the way to climb the fell—and the way to return. It is the only example in this book where the walk goes out and back by the same route. Alternatives are available but are frankly not as good as the original.

However, Harter Fell is of modest height so the climb can be combined with a walk along the Esk from the car park at Dalegarth

WALK 19: Muncaster Fell and The River Esk

Map: English Lakes (SW) 1:25,000.
Start: MR086965. The Ravenglass Station on the Ravenglass and Eskdale Railway. See alternatives in text—the walk is infinitely variable.
Distance: The complete walk is $10^1/_2$ miles (17km) from Dalegarth Station to Ravenglass Station including Stanley Ghyll and Muncaster Castle grounds.
Time: 5 hrs.
What's it Like?: There's a bit of everything in this walk: railways, waterfalls, fellwalking and a country house. Superb for springtime flowers. It can easily be broken up into separate parts, thanks to Ratty, if you don't feel like tackling the whole. Nothing strenuous, but there's a steepish climb right at the very end in Muncaster Park, so be warned! Muncaster Fell can be rather boggy.
Shorter Alternatives: (1) Stanley Ghyll Force—$1^1/_2$hrs; (2) Along the riverside to Doctor Bridge, returning along the other bank and crossing the stepping stones; can be joined to (1) above—1hr; (3) walk along the riverbank downstream to Forge Bridge and so to Eskdale Green Station—1hr; can be joined to either or both of (1) and (2) above; (4) to Devoke Water, the largest tarn in Lakeland, but not an inspiring place for all that. A good track all the way and return the same way—$5^1/_2$ miles (9km) (See text).
Bad Weather Alternatives: (1) Muncaster Castle and grounds—bird gardens, nature trail, garden centre and even a teenagers' commando course! (2) two water mills—at Muncaster Mill (096977) which has its own station on the Ratty line and Eskdale Mill (176012) which is at Boot, a short walk from Dalegarth Station.

La'al Ratty, a Botanist's Paradise and a Panorama

There can't be many visitors to the Lake District who have never heard of the celebrated narrow gauge railway up Eskdale from the coast at Ravenglass, known affectionately

Above: **The central fells of Lakeland seen from Ross's Camp on Muncaster Fell. Harter Fell can be seen on the right, the long valley of the Esk, the great pyramid of Bowfell in the centre and Scafell on the left with Kirkfell peeping over its shoulder.**

Left: La'al Ratty, the famous Ravenglass and Eskdale Railway which can be used on this walk. The train is standing in Dalegarth Station, Eskdale.

Middle: The stepping stones across the Esk at Dalegarth and the church of St. Catherine.

Right: The approach to Stanley Gill is through a delightful ravine.

as La'al Ratty. La'al is Cumbrian for little, so the name is appropriate because the width of the gauge is only 15 inches and the line is just 7 miles (11km) long. Six perfect miniature steam locos (and a similar number of diesels) maintain a service between six stations, with a mixture of open and closed carriages. It connects with British Rail at Ravenglass and its proper name is the Ravenglass and Eskdale Railway.

La'al Ratty—where the Ratty came from nobody seems certain—was originally built to a wider gauge in 1875 and has had a chequered career since then as various mines and quarries which used the line opened and closed, but its future as a popular tourist attraction now seems assured. It is a boon for anyone wishing to walk the lower Esk valley and full use is made of it in the walk described here.

Because of Ratty there are four different ways in which this walk can be done; starting at either end you can ride out and walk back or *vice versa*. Similarly, using intermediate stations, you can shorten it. Long or short, it is pre-eminently a spring walk because of the wide variety of flowers—and not all of them wild, as we shall see.

Having walked the route in both directions I prefer to take the Ratty up the valley and walk

downstream to the sea. It is true that this way you miss the sudden impact of the view from Hooker Crag of the Lakeland fells—one of the most breathtaking panoramas—but there's a certain satisfaction in reaching a seashore at the end of the day; there's nothing so final as a sandy beach.

So take the Ratty from Ravenglass, sit back in the open carriage and let the magnificent scenery sweep past, whilst the engine chuffs away valiantly and gives a toot at every bend. Travel to the end of the line, to Dalegarth Station, where there is a tearoom and a fine view of Harter Fell: in appearance every inch a mountaineer's mountain. A few yards up the road from the station a small lane leads off to St Catherine's Church, a tiny chapel resting in idyllic surroundings by the riverside. As a foundation it goes back to the days of antiquity, but the present building is a Victorian restoration of 1881.

When the river is low the stepping stones by the church present no difficulties, but after heavy rain the water rushes round them in menacing fashion. There's no other way across, however, unless you fancy a long walk upstream to Doctor Bridge—or rather, there *is* a way, but not one to be recommended. A few yards upstream there's all that remains of an old bridge; two iron girders across a chasm with the river rushing below a long way down. Incidentally, the Esk is noted for its delectable bathing pools, deep and green amidst the rocks, and nowhere more so than the stretch between Doctor Bridge and the church. The pink granite for which the valley was once famous shows up well in the river bed, too.

On the other side of the stepping stones a gate leads into a meadow and a path runs parallel with the stream until it meets a broad bridleway climbing up the fellside. You can in fact follow this track to Devoke Water, the largest of Lakeland's tarns, about 3 miles (5km) away, but we turn off through a gate marked 'To Waterfalls' within a few yards and pass through a conifer wood to a stream called Stanley Ghyll. The Stanleys own the adjacent Dalegarth Hall and Ghyll was thought in Victorian times to be much more romantic than *gill,* which is the proper spelling!

In no time at all the path leads into a narrow gorge and across a bridge. This in turn leads to a second bridge and then a third from where a view can be got of a great gushing spout of water, 60ft (18m) high, pouring into the canyon. This is Stanley Force, once known as Dalegarth Force, though that name seems out of fashion nowadays. The view is partly hidden by the many shrubs and trees which grow out of the gorge and there is a footpath beyond the bridge which leads nearer to the waterfall, but it is a perilous place suitable only for mountain goats. Instead, if you retreat down the gorge a few paces a way can be seen leading off to the left up numerous steps and by following these, and another leftwards path at the top of the steps, you will come out onto a startling balcony which gives dizzying views of the gorge. Beware! The edge is quite unguarded and it is a sheer drop—lie on your tummy and look over if you must. It is not the place for dogs or young children.

A few yards back from the drop there's a stile leading out of the trees to the open fellside where once again we meet the Devoke Water track. It's a grand walk down this bridle-path, with impressive views across the vale to Burnmoor and Scafell so that before you realise it, you are back again at the entrance gate. Dalegarth Station can be reached in about fifteen minutes by returning to the stepping stones from here, if anyone feels they've done enough walking for one day! The trip so far will have taken a leisurely hour and a half, scarcely more.

To continue the walk, however, is simply a matter of following the path opposite the waterfall's gate. It leads behind Dalegarth Hall, built by the Stanleys about 1599 and celebrated for its round chimneys, which show up well from our vantage point. The hall was originally larger than at present, but much of it was pulled down in 1750 when it had long ceased to be the principal residence of the family. The path through the woods is very clear with one confusing junction where the right decision is to stay in the woods and keep near the stream. In spring, there's an abundance of wild flowers including the yellow gorse in profusion. At Milkingsteads, the path goes through a field and past a footbridge then, quite suddenly, bursts out onto the road at Forge Bridge.

Across the river, happily on our line of march, is the King George IV inn where there is a chance to partake of modest refreshment if you time it right. We could call it 'last chance corner' I suppose, for the hard work still lies ahead and there's no further respite. Just past here too, up the hill a bit, is Eskdale Green Station on the Ratty, which is the last chance to cop out before things get tougher. If you abandon the walk here it will probably be two and a half hours since you left Dalegarth Station—but that depends how long you spent in the King George!

A footpath leads beside the railway for a bit then through a gate and round a copse to cross a large field which the map calls Forge Hills. Sheep and cattle browse in the field and the Esk flows in the valley below, all slow and twisting and backed by the fells around Devoke Water. To the north, the village of Eskdale Green stands out prettily against the massed dark trees of Miterdale and the distant blue mountains.

Visitors can look down on Stanley Force from this exposed ledge. (Photo: Duncan Unsworth).

In the height of summer Stanley Ghyll looks almost tropical.
(Photo: Duncan Unsworth).

At the far side of the field there is a footpath crossroads with an indicator pointing this way and that, but our road is clear enough. A long slanting trod cuts across the fell which rises amiably before us and seems to lead to better things and this is the way we must go. It looks as though a well-made, broad path is to take us across Muncaster Fell and so for the most part it proves. It also proves to be uncommonly boggy even in the driest weather so if you are wearing trainers—and this walk can easily be done in such footwear—you need to be a bit nimble at times to avoid getting your feet wet.

The path leads enchantingly round hummocks and through little valleys to a gateway in a drystone wall beyond which is a curious rock table so obviously of Stone Age origin that it comes as a shock to find someone's pulling our leg. Carved on the slab are the words 'Ross's Camp 1883': it commemorates a Victorian shooting party who raised it as a luncheon table.

But Ross and his mates knew what they were about for the table is in a glorious setting. Miterdale and Eskdale look very fine from here and there is a panorama which includes almost the whole of the major Lakeland fells. It really is one of the best viewpoints in the area, though half a mile on at Hooker Crag, where the summit Ordnance Survey column is found, it might be considered better still. The height is only 758ft (231m), but the view includes Pillar, Scafell, Bowfell, Coniston Old Man, Black Combe and everything in between. Most astonishingly of all, out to sea like Treasure Island is the Isle of Man, so close you feel you could almost touch it.

The Ravenglass estuary lies like a map below and wooded hills roll down to the sea

obscuring the castle and village. Further over, however, there is quite a different prospect: the towers and domes of the Sellafield nuclear plant. A king once hid in those woods; I wonder what Henry VI would think if he saw the coast today?

From Hooker Crag the path leads swiftly down to a lane hemmed in by thickets of rhododendron, denser than they are in their native Nepal. In the midst of the thickets, hidden from common gaze and approached by an unmarked path, is the forlorn-looking Muncaster Tarn. It is really quite a sizeable sheet of water, with islands to boot, but it is so hedged about by the rhododendrons that it looks less like a Lakeland tarn than a backwater of the Amazon.

Fell Lane, broad and straight as an arrow, leads down to the corner of the main road (A595) by Muncaster Castle. The quickest way now is to walk down the main road to the station, which is exactly a mile away, but a walk like this is better ended on a high note, even if it takes a bit longer. So walk up the hill to where a sign points across the road to Muncaster Church and go down the lane past the church and into the grounds of Muncaster Castle. The lane is lined with splendid rhododendrons—not the massed overgrown plants of Muncaster Fells, but a dazzling variety of choice specimens. In fact, Muncaster Castle, which is the home of the Penningtons, is famous for its rhododendrons.

The castle and grounds are open to the public, but a public footpath actually goes right through the kiddies' adventure playground and climbs steeply through more rhododendron woods, carpeted with bluebells in season, to emerge onto a bald open fell with no footpath. The Isle of Man looks positively menacing from here, like a huge grey battleship standing offshore and you head towards it until, round the shoulder of the hill, it is possible to drop down to a gateway and farm track which leads past the cottage at Newtown.

Soon the lane becomes a hardtop. It goes through woods which shelter all sorts of plants, including uncommon grasses, and in which is found Walls Castle, the remains of a bath-house and reputed to be the highest standing Roman walls left in Britain. Shortly after this a narrow track leads off to the left under what must be the lowest railway tunnel in the world, where tall men duck and even short men feel uncomfortable. Beyond it lies the beach and the way to the main street of Ravenglass and a well-found pint in the Ratty Arms.

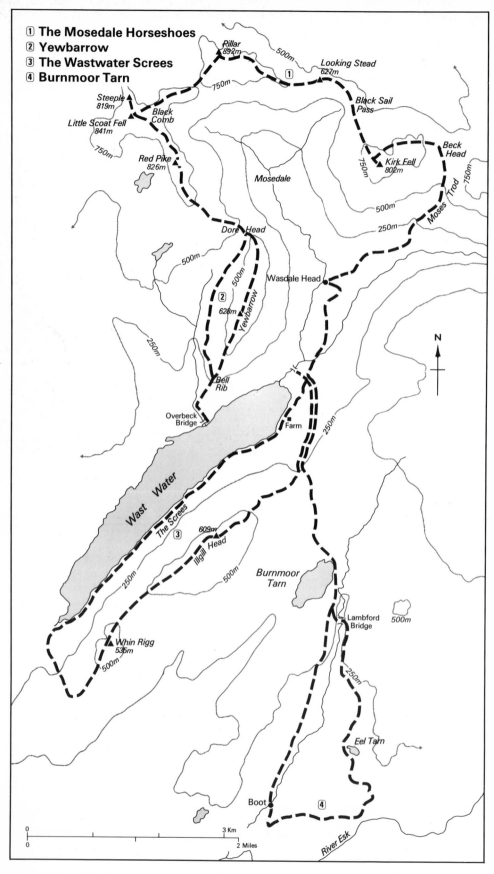

① **The Mosedale Horseshoes**
② **Yewbarrow**
③ **The Wastwater Screes**
④ **Burnmoor Tarn**

Pillar
892m

Looking Stead
627m

500m

①

Steeple
819m

Black
Comb

Black Sail
Pass

Little Scoat Fell
841m

Beck
Head

750m

Kirk Fell
802m

Red Pike
826m

750m

Moses Trod

750m

Mosedale

500m

Dore Head

250m

500m

Wasdale Head

②

628m

500m

Yewbarrow

250m

N

Bell
Rib

Overbeck
Bridge

Farm

250m

Wast   Water

The Screes

609m

③

Illgill Head

500m

Burnmoor
Tarn

250m

Lambford
Bridge

500m

Whin Rigg
535m

500m

250m

Eel Tarn

Boot

④

0   3 Km
0   2 Miles

River Esk

84

WALK 20: The Wast Water Screes

Above: **Looking back along the bracken slopes at the start of the traverse. From the centre of the picture the walk goes round the lake past Wasdale Head Hall Farm which can be seen quite clearly.**

Map: English Lakes (SW) 1:25,000.
Start: MR182074. Car park at Wasdale Head.
Distance: 8¹/₂ miles (14km).
Time: 5hrs.
What's it Like?: The crossing of the Screes is a unique experience. Not long but fairly arduous. Good balance required and boots are advisable to avoid a twisted ankle or worse. In bad weather the crossing would be purgatory. The rest of the walk is easy, with good views.
Shorter Alternative: Reverse the walk to Illgill Head and Whin Rigg returning the same way— 7¹/₂ miles (12km), 3¹/₂hrs.
Bad Weather Alternatives: In Wasdale? You must be joking!

Along the Shore of the Deepest Lake

The great fans of scree which shoot down the southern side of Wast Water are amongst the most awe-inspiring scenes in the British moun-

tains. They are concentrated at the western end of the shore where a line of huge black crags separated by chasm-like gullies marks the ridge of Whin Rigg and Illgill Head, the mountains on this side of the lake. It is from these crags that the great scree slopes descend, straight down into the water, at the critical angle of rest, 35°–40°. The slopes actually continue to the bottom of the lake, 258ft (79m) below the surface, thereby creating a continuous scree slope of some 2000ft (600m). Perhaps only in the Isle of Skye will one find scree slopes of similar magnitude, and none of those can match the grandeur of Wast Water.

They are best seen from across the water, where the narrow motor road comes down to the lake shore. Only from that position can the full panoply of crags and gullies be seen, towering above the scree itself. It looks like a major climbing ground, but it isn't—the rock is

pretty poor. There are a couple of long gully climbs, one of which caused the great Victorian alpinist A.F. Mummery to condemn climbing at Wasdale Head as both difficult and dangerous.

Certainly the Screes look too difficult and dangerous for a fellwalker to tackle and yet a keen eye can discern the tenuous thread of a path across the lower part of the steep slopes. Can it be possible? Indeed it can.

The walk begins at the head of the lake where there is a camp site and car park. A bridleway leads across the Lingmell Gill (we shall arrive back at this point at the end of the walk) and immediately veers off towards the water's edge which it follows until it suddenly turns inland to Wasdale Head Hall Farm. At this point a smaller track goes through a gate and continues along the shore. The way ahead seems particularly uninteresting at this stage— just steep slopes, covered with bracken in the season.

The path becomes a narrow swathe through the knee-high ferns, climbs well above the lake and suddenly one is conscious of considerable exposure. The slopes are exceedingly steep, the path exceedingly narrow and one slip will undoubtedly send you tumbling into England's deepest lake.

Here and there the path has collapsed a little, but nothing to worry about and for the most part it is a very sound little path, well graded and gravelled by nature. Where it meets the first scree shoots it is actually wider and one could stroll along whistling cheerfully, hands in pockets. Make the most of it. Eat some nourishing food, see that your buttons are secure and your rucksack is fastened, for you are in for a very tough time indeed.

The ferny banks reappear, but the scree becomes more frequent and bigger. Where once it had been the size of hazel nuts, it now becomes the size of coconuts. The pieces get bigger still and the path breaks up as everyone chooses their own way through the mass of steep stones. There comes a point (I am sure everyone experiences it) where you suddenly realise you are standing on a very steep slope of loose stones, any or all of which seem likely to slide into the lake at any moment, carrying you with them! Sometimes they *do* slide, but I've never heard of anyone being caught. Nevertheless, you have to watch your step—you can start a minor landslide or even twist your ankle.

The going is very rough for a while but then it eases. There is time now to look at the scenery—especially towards the valley head where Yewbarrow, Kirk Fell and Great Gable form a magnificent mountain backcloth. On a still summer's evening the reflections of the mountains in the water of the lake can be like

Wastwater and the Screes from the western end. (Photo: Duncan Unsworth).

The path at the end of the Screes comes as a great relief. (Photo: Duncan Unsworth).

something from a Chinese painting.

It is tempting to look *up* the slope you are balancing across, too, but the view is disappointing; a dizzy uniform tilt of stones and the merest hint of the crags above. The best crags are near the end of the lake, but even so, the foreshortening makes them seem insignificant.

Round about this point—just when you think the whole excursion is rather exaggerated as to difficulty, the Screes suddenly trap you. By the time you see it coming it is too late. You are faced with one final, horrendous, slope of scree; large blocks defying gravity in teetering piles and stretching, so it seems, to the end of the lake. Either you go on or, perish the thought, you go back across all that scree you've already crossed. It seems easier to go on.

It is slow, laborious work. Progress seems infinitesimal and time slips by at an accelerated pace. It is also very arduous—not too bad perhaps if you've started fresh from Wasdale Head that morning, but if you've come over from Eskdale on Walk 21, you might be feeling the strain. There is no path, of course, but long before the end of the torture you can see where the path starts again; so near and yet so far. It is the most sadistic slope of scree in the kingdom.

But all good things must come to an end! The lake narrows to a small estuary and a path runs along the shore to a pumping station beyond which there is an access road. A little way along this there is a gate and by turning left here it is possible to climb up by the side of the curious gully known as Greathall Gill, to the ridge above. The climb is about 1000ft (305m) and it is quite steep, but it is the last hard work of the day.

Perhaps the greatest surprise for anyone not in the know already, is the complete contrast between the side of the ridge facing Wast Water and the opposite side facing Burnmoor and Miterdale. The first is steep and rocky, as we already have good reason to know, but the other just slopes away towards Eskdale in unbroken sweeps of grass. Our walk continues along the top of the ridge, first over Whin Rigg (1755ft/535m) then for a gently rising mile or so to Illgill Head (1998ft (609m)—the highest point is beyond the trig block! By keeping near the edge of the crags (but not too near!) there are dramatic glimpses of the Screes and the lake and from the summit a fine view of Wasdale Head, framed by its majestic mountains.

Beyond Illgill Head it is easy to take any line down the steepish grass slopes to the well-seen track across Burnmoor and head either for Eskdale (Walk 21) or back to Wasdale. For the latter the path is steep, broad and rocky, down past some ruined cottages to the car park.

WALK 21: Burnmoor Tarn

Map: English Lakes (SW) 1:25,000.
Start: MR 190010. The Woolpack Inn on the valley road.
Best Access: In view of the return to Boot it is probably better to park a car in the Dalegarth Station car park (MR173007) and walk along the road, or more attractively, by way of the river bank to the inn. (see the start of Walk 19).
Distance: To the tarn and back 5 miles (8km); to Wasdale Head Inn 5¹/2 miles (9km); to Wasdale Head Inn and back to Boot 10¹/2 miles (17km). These distances do not include the mile or so between the car park and the Woolpack.
Time: To the tarn and back 2¹/2 hrs; to Wasdale Head Inn 3hrs.
Links with Other Walks: The walk can be joined to Walk 20.
What's it Like?: A delightful moorland walk, a bit boggy underfoot but not arduous or long. In misty weather the track would be difficult to follow and one would then prefer the broader track from Boot.
Shorter Alternatives: (1) As far as Eel Tarn and back—a leisurely hour; (2) Dalegarth Force (see Walk 19); (3) Any of the riverside walks between Doctor Bridge (MR189007) and Forge Bridge (MR149995) (See Walk 19).
Bad Weather Alternatives: (1) Take the train to Ravenglass where there is Muncaster Castle, with bird sanctuary, nature trail, garden centre *et al*; world famous rhododendrons in season, (2) There are two water mills: Muncaster Mill (MR096977) and Eskdale Mill (MR176012).

Above: **The descent from Burnmoor into Wasdale Head. In the background is Kirk Fell (left) and Great Gable (right).**

Across the Moors between Eskdale and Wasdale

I first crossed Burnmoor (or Eskdale Moor, to give it its proper name) when I was fourteen years old and at once felt an affinity with its

Above left: **Burnmoor seen from Birker Moor. The large mountain towering over the moor is Scafell and in the background is the Pillar group.**

Above right: **Burnmoor Tarn.**

open spaces and lonely tarns. It isn't a dramatic place like Gable or Pillar; it doesn't even have particularly dramatic surroundings like those you get on Birker Moor, for instance, but it does have an indefinable quality all of its own.

The moor can be used as the best of all ways between Eskdale and Wasdale, and a pleasant day can be spent walking from one to the other in the morning in time for lunch and walking back in time for dinner. If lunch is somewhat liquid the return journey seems to fly, though it is long enough to complete the sobering-up process, thus allowing a fresh start in the evening! Most people find this an admirable arrangement.

Alternatively, the walk can be done to the tarn and back from Eskdale; a nice easy stroll. Curiously enough, from Wasdale it has less charm as a walk—the upward path is too brutal and there's none of the mystery you get in the other direction. Finally, this walk can be combined with Walk 20—but beware! The path along the Screes is a very different kettle of fish from the gentle path over Burnmoor.

The walk starts at the Woolpack Inn, about a mile up the valley from Dalegarth Station. (See Walk 19). A short lane runs down the left hand side of the Inn and carries on round the

back to a small wicket gate marked 'footpath' which gives directly onto the fell.

The path climbs up into a minor wonderland of rocky outcrops. Unlike many Lakeland paths, this one is hardly worn at all, partly no doubt because it is lined with the hard-wearing pink granite which is Eskdale's own rock, and partly because it seems to have fallen into disuse in recent years; this is not a place for the hordes, thank goodness. Clear enough at first, there are places further on where the path requires the diligence of an Indian scout.

There are little grassy dells between the outcrops and the path follows these, dodging in and out until it passes a ruined bothy and suddenly there is a fine little tarn, Eel Tarn. Over to the right the Scafell range rises as a long barren ridge, the most uninteresting side of this grand mountain, though there's a glimpse of something finer, a pointed peak which might be Scafell Pike or Esk Pike— anyway it's a long way off. To the left is the long broad valley of the Whillan Beck which comes down from Burnmoor Tarn, and beyond it the swelling turf rising up to Whin Rigg and Illgill Head. Looking at these two fells from this side, nobody could imagine the savage splendour of their north faces.

The path leads round the tarn then sweeps

out in a broad curve round the lower flanks of Eskdale Fell to Lambford Bridge. It isn't always clear, though here and there white crosses have been marked on some of the larger boulders (mostly for the benefit of walkers coming the other way, it seems to me!). Patches of bog enliven the journey.

Lambford Bridge is no longer the simple plank it once was in my youth. It has been replaced by a substantial affair where you can pause and watch the Whillan Beck flow past. On the far side there is no path at all: lots of bog and a stiff little pull up the hill to the main track which runs across the moor from Boot in Eskdale to Wasdale Head.

This path was a famous corpse road, of which there are several in the Lakes. They are so called because corpses from outlying hamlets were carried along them to the parish church for burial—in this case, from Wasdale Head to the church of St Catherine in Eskdale. As you can imagine, there are various stories about runaway horses carrying off corpses which were never seen again, except in spectral form. At night you cross this moor in peril of boggarts! The story I like best though, is that of the woman being carried across the moor in her coffin when the horse caught it against a rowan tree. The magic properties of the rowan (a sacred tree since Norse days) flowed into the corpse and revived her. A few years later she died again and her body began its second journey to Eskdale, led by the woman's son. The parting advice from the bereaved husband was 'Tak care o' yon rowan, John!'

Burnmoor Tarn appears shyly peeping through a gap in the moorland ridges. It is best to leave the main path and go over to the tarn where there is another path teetering round the very edge. A herd of black cattle stand in the shallows at the Bulatt Bridge end and the scene is like something by Landseer. The tarn is very big—almost as big as Devoke Water—and very still. To get the best views you should walk round by Bulatt Bridge to the far side where little streams ribbon themselves on entering the tarn. The tarn, the moor and the distant shape of Birker Moor make a magnificent scene.

All the way across the moor the tops of Kirk Fell, Yewbarrow and the Pillar group have been on the horizon to the north, the lower parts cut off by a long low ridge of moor stretching between Illgill Head and Scafell. From the tarn the track climbs the ridge, revealing more of the fells at every step. There's a curious large stone compound here and over on the right of the track is the site of

Burnmoor Tarn. (Photo: Duncan Unsworth).

Maiden Castle where the commoners of Wasdale, Eskdale and Miterdale would meet in May at Beltan time, a ceremony dating from antiquity. As the crest is passed the valley head comes into view and the lake of Wast Water. Impressive fells, steep-sided and rocky, rise from the valley floor.

The path goes down very steeply to the valley, broad now and full of rough stones underfoot. Two ancient dwellings now in ruins are passed and then it's down to the club hut at Brackenclose and the camp site. It's a further mile, either by road or path, to the pub.

Of all the hotels in Lakeland, the Wasdale Head Inn is the one with the closest connections with the mountaineering fraternity. This is where rock-climbing started in Britain; the fame of the place perpetuated by stories of Old Will Ritson, the nineteenth-century landlord who could hold his own with the best of them. 'Why don't you go in London to see the sights, Will?' some southern gentlemen demanded. 'I've noan a need,' replied Will, 'when some on 'em comes up here to see me.'

The little church is worth a visit, if only to see the graves of those killed on the surrounding crags. 'The mountains give, and the mountains take', said Don Whillans, one of the best of British climbers. Wasdale shows this clearly.

The way back follows the same route as far as the tarn and proves a stiff pull out of the valley though it's downhill from there. Stride along the Corpse Road. Ahead there is a glorious panorama with the rocky triangle of Harter Fell, as always, dominating Eskdale so completely. There are many who regard this fell as the most beautiful in the Lake District, and not without reason.

The path descends swiftly into the hamlet of Boot, a short distance from where it began.

WALK 22: Yewbarrow

Above: **On the summit ridge of Yewbarrow. Wastwater can be seen on the right and Burnmoor Tarn on the left.** (Photo: Duncan Unsworth).

Map: English Lakes (SW) 1:25,000.
Start: MR168068. Car park at Overbeck Bridge, Wasdale.
Distance: 4 miles (6km).
Time: 3$^{1}/_{2}$hrs.
What's it Like?: Short and sharp. Both the ascent and descent involve steep scrambling. The degree of difficulty is hard to assess; more difficult than Striding Edge or Sharp Edge and perhaps equal to Jack's Rake *technically*—but there isn't the exposure these other routes have and that makes a big difference. Not a route for the nervous.
Links with Other Walks: From Dore Head the walk can be continued over the Mosedale Horseshoe. See Walk 23.
Shorter Alternatives: (1) Walk up the Overbeck valley to Dore Head and back, 2hrs; (2) Follow the magnificent valley of the Nether Beck up to Scoat Tarn. Start from MR158063, where there is adequate roadside parking. 6-mile (10km) round trip of about 3$^{1}/_{2}$hrs in wild, little-frequented country. Not shorter than Yewbarrow, but no scrambling involved.
Bad Weather Alternative: Visit the little church at Wasdale Head, the Barndoor Shop and the pub, if it is open.

The Toughest Little Walk in Lakeland

Yewbarrow sticks out into Wasdale like a sore thumb and in so doing manages to dominate the scene. If you look up the valley from the lakeside road, or even more so from the Wasdale Screes, it is not the grand mountains of Pillar, Scafell or Gable which dominate the scene, but Yewbarrow, much smaller and unknown to all but the dedicated fellwalker. It isn't until you draw level with Yewbarrow on the road and foreshortening diminishes its presence that the crags of Scafell above Hollow Stones and the bulk of Great Gable and the

thin ribbon of the Styhead Pass start to take over the scene.

From the car park at Overbeck Bridge, where the walk starts, Yewbarrow looks steep and difficult. It is. It is the toughest little walk in Lakeland, and even the great Baddeley, whose guidebook was the Bible of the early fellwalkers, admits to not knowing Yewbarrow. Some of his successors are a bit vague on the subject, too!

So although this is a short walk, suitable for an afternoon, it is not for the inexperienced. A degree of scrambling ability is needed, and should you go wrong and depart from the proper way, which is easily done, you need to be able to extricate yourself. This is not a bad weather climb nor a place for children unless they are properly trained, tough little brats.

From the car park at Overbeck Bridge a small but distinct path leads up the beck for a short way then turns up by a fence and starts the direct climb of the broad grassy rib which is such a notable feature of the fell. It is a steep slog but mercifully short, ending at a stile which leads over the fence and onto the fell below the Yewbarrow crags. The path forks almost immediately and the upper fork leads towards a distinct buttress of clean rock called Dropping Crag, better known to climbers as Overbeck Buttress. Soon the path reaches a scree shoot, level with the foot of the buttress.

This is the first opportunity to go wrong so it is worth having a good look round. The path has virtually disappeared, but there are faint traces across the scree to the foot of the buttress and a good path there, leading out of sight round the rocks. That is *not* the way unless you fancy yourself as a 'rock-jock'. Up above there is a jumble of rocks and on the right the bigger crags of Bell Rib, which looks like the summit of Yewbarrow but isn't. A gully, evil-looking and probably wet, comes down through the broken rocks towards the scree and disagreeable though it may seem, this is the way—or at least, it indicates the way. By going up the scree a bit a path is met *which is cairned:* by following the cairns and using common sense a way is found into and out of the gully, up rock ribs, across ledges and gradually but inexorably to the grassy belvedere well above Overbeck Buttress. It is a fascinating scramble because the route has to be worked out at almost every step of the way.

When you break out of the gully it is surprising to see how much of the climb still lies ahead. Very steep grassy slopes broken here and there by small outcrops rise to a crest line towards which a path of sorts picks its

The top of Overbeck Buttress, passed on the climb up. The route comes up the slopes on the left, very steeply.

way. The end is sudden and dramatic. You step onto a narrow col which plunges down on the other side towards Wasdale Head. On the right is a rock outcrop, the top of Bell Rib and on the left another rocky outcrop. This col is called Great Door.

With a little care it is easy to climb the rocks to the top of Bell Rib and survey the whole of Wasdale, stretched out like a map. Across the lake, too, can be seen Burnmoor, like a green baize tablecloth, with its tarn a dark round stain.

From Great Door it is easy to scramble up the rocks on the main crest line towards the summit. Once above the outcrop the ridge becomes quite wide and surprisingly boggy for such a rocky fell. A path leads to the undistinguished summit cairn (2060ft/628m).

Yewbarrow is full of surprises and another is the realisation of what a long ridge it forms— over a mile from Bell Rib to the other end, Stirrup Crag. The walking is easy, the ridge rising to another summit adorned by two cairns. It is the end of the mountain. In front is the ridge leading to Red Pike and the dark, gloomy head of Mosedale; Black Crag, Wind Gap and Pillar. There are fewer scenes more desolate in the entire Lake District.

Suddenly you are aware that between you and the onward ridges there is a very big drop. Stirrup Crag does not belie its name—it really is a crag, down which the path creeps from ledge to ledge, using little grooves and chimneys. It is scrambling of the best sort, tricky in a couple of places, but not particularly exposed. A firm grip and a steady head are the main prerequisites, though a bit of balance won't come amiss either! It is the climax of the walk and you end at the broad saddle called Dore Head with a feeling of exhilaration tinged with a little relief.

The return to the car park down Over Beck is simplicity itself; a gentle end to a strenuous afternoon. The path is indistinct at first but it improves lower down and eventually brings you back to the stile below Bell Rib. There are lovely views down the valley; Bowderdale, the lake, the Screes and out towards the coast. Then it goes steeply down, straight into the car park.

Left: **Yewbarrow from below.**

93

WALK 23: The Mosedale Horseshoe

Map: English Lakes (NW) 1:25,000. Unfortunately the Inn, Yewbarrow and Overbeck are just off this map and so you need the SW sheet as well for complete coverage—but they are not absolutely essential.

Start: (1) MR168068. Car park at Overbeck Bridge; or (2) MR186087. Wasdale Head Inn.

Distance: Little Mosedale 9¹/₂ miles (15km), with Kirk Fell 11 miles (18km). The direct approach to Dore Head from Wasdale saves 3 miles (5km) on the day.

Time: 7-8hrs.

What's it Like?: Perhaps the finest of all the valley head walks, it is a fairly arduous undertaking though with no real technical difficulty. Dangerous ground in bad weather because of the many crags which surround the ridges.

Links with Other Walks: Yewbarrow (Walk 22) makes a logical start to this horseshoe, but adds considerably to the difficulty and the time required. Add at least 2hrs. Strong walkers only should attempt the Big Mosedale.

Shorter Alternatives: (1) The ascent of Kirk Fell by Black Sail Pass—Kirk Fell can be traversed, with a descent via Gavel Neese (see text); (2) Pillar by the High Level Route. From Wasdale climb Black Sail Pass and just beyond Looking Stead take an almost horizontal path on the Ennerdale side to a prominent cairn, Robinson's Cairn. Beyond this descend into a slight hollow then climb up to the start of the Shamrock Traverse. Cross this to the Rescue Box and follow the path steeply up to the summit of Pillar. The route gives fine views of the famous Pillar Rock. In clear weather there are no dangers but it should be avoided in mist or bad weather. The return from the summit is along the ridge back to Black Sail Pass. 7 miles (11km), over 2500ft (750m) of ascent. About 5hrs.

Bad Weather Alternative: None!

Above: **The view north from Kirk Fell. The Pillar ridge is in the foreground and the High Stile ridge in the centre. In the distance is Grasmoor and the Coledale Peaks.** (Photo: Duncan Unsworth).

Black Sail Pass. (Photo: Duncan Unsworth).

A Tough Walk Around the Pillar Massif

Mosedale is a small valley branching north from Wasdale Head and surrounded by a ring of high, steep-sided mountains. The Mosedale Horseshoe is one of the best-known ridge walks in the Lake District: an old-time test piece that once had the distinction of being the subject of a television play. It has a reputation for being one of the harder of the standard ridge walks, and done in its entirety it probably is. However, the walk can be shortened in various ways and still provide an interesting route. As nobody seems certain these days as to what exactly the walk consists of I would like to suggest that two alternatives be considered, which we can call the Big Mosedale and the Little Mosedale.

The Big Mosedale encompasses the entire valley—and perhaps a bit more. It takes in Yewbarrow, Red Pike, Scoat Fell, Black Crag, Pillar, Looking Stead and Kirk Fell. The Little Mosedale is the same but leaving out Yewbarrow and Kirk Fell; that is to say, the ridge between Dore Head and Black Sail Pass, encompassing the head of the valley. Many people will find this a sufficient walk, but Kirk Fell can be added without too much fatigue. Yewbarrow, however, is a different matter entirely—see Walk 22.

Even before you start, a decision has to be made whether to take the gentle approach to Dore Head from the car park at Overbeck Bridge and add three miles to the day's outing, or whether to take the short, brutal slopes up the col from the sheep-fold in Mosedale. This saves a couple of miles at the end of the day, but is a violent start to the walk. The Wasdale Head camp site is halfway between the two and if you are starting from there then Overbeck is the wiser choice.

From the car park at Overbeck Bridge the way follows the stream for a short distance then turns uphill to follow the broad green rib which is such a distinctive feature of Yewbarrow. It climbs steeply to a ladder stile which leads onto the fellside below the Yewbarrow crags where there is a path which soon divides, one path climbing up to Yewbarrow and a lower path contouring round the fellside. On the right the ragged crest of Yewbarrow seems almost near enough to touch whilst on the left, across the valley, are the outcrops of Red Pike. The path climbs very gradually and towards the end becomes less distinct and harder to follow.

Dore Head proves to be a broad col sheltering under Stirrup Crag, which is the northern end of Yewbarrow. On the far side you can look over into Mosedale and assess the alternative approach, where a badly eroded scree slope plunges into the valley. The ascent avoids the scree, climbing the grass to the side, but it is very steep.

From Dore Head too can be seen the dark brooding crags at the head of Mosedale and the long white streak of scree that is Wind Gap. Our route is approximately towards the crest as seen and we start by climbing Red Pike, winding in between the outcrops which grace this aspect of the fell. It is a fairly gentle climb but the summit (2909ft/886m) is dramatic; it lies right on the edge of the great crags plunging down into Mosedale.

Following the ridge an easy half-mile or so leads to Scoat Fell (2759ft/841m) which the Ordnance Survey insists is called Little Scoat Fell although it is 128ft (39m) higher than the neighbouring summit they call Great Scoat Fell! From here to Pillar, and indeed beyond, the scenery is magnificently wide-sweeping.

A wall runs along the ridge towards Black Crag but soon peters out. Boulders give way to a grassy belvedere across the top of the latter (2716ft/828m) then comes a steep descent into a conspicuous nick in the ridge, a real Tyrolean *scharte,* called Wind Gap. On the Mosedale side there's an appalling scree slope—and a path. I once flogged up it with a full rucksack many years ago and I still remember it as one of the most arduous ascents in Lakeland. From the gap a steep, rough ascent marked by cairns leads to the summit of Pillar (2927ft/

892m). The summit area is large with a number of cairns and the trig block. The views are widespread with the great sugarloaf top of Gable dominating the scene to the south-east.

From the top of Pillar following the ridge along to the Black Sail Pass is easy and a broad path descends the pass into Mosedale and along the little valley floor to Wasdale Head.

To take in Kirk Fell as well—and perhaps one should, because it is there—the way scrambles up the rocky path from Black Sail Pass which soon eases and leads across the broad top to the cairn at 2631ft (802m), overlooking the steep Wasdale slopes of the mountain. It is feasible to descend from here straight down the slopes south-west, but the way is abominably steep and not at all good for knees which might already be fairly tired. It is better to cross the fell to its secondary summit, then scramble down Rib End to the tarn at Beck Head and follow the famous Moses Trod around the flanks of Great Gable to the top of Gavel Neese, a grass rib which points like an arrow to the valley. This too is steep, but not as steep nor as long as the direct way down Kirk Fell. Either way leads directly back to Wasdale Head.

Autumn in Mosedale. Pillar forms the skyline and the steep screes of Wind Gap can be seen.

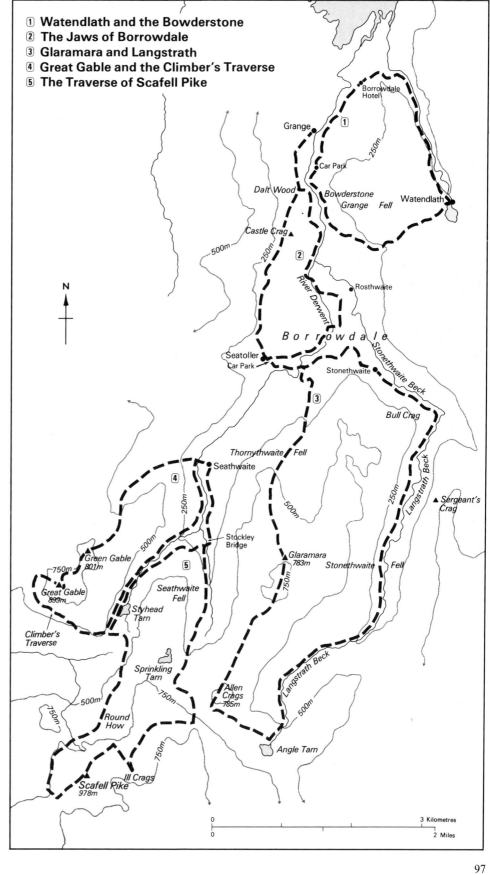

1. **Watendlath and the Bowderstone**
2. **The Jaws of Borrowdale**
3. **Glaramara and Langstrath**
4. **Great Gable and the Climber's Traverse**
5. **The Traverse of Scafell Pike**

Borrowdale Hotel

Grange

Car Park

Dalt Wood

Bowderstone
Grange Fell

Watendlath

Castle Crag ▲

250m

500m

River Derwent

Rosthwaite

B o r r o w d a l e

Stonethwaite Beck

Seatoller
Car Park

Stonethwaite

Bull Crag

Thornythwaite Fell

Seathwaite

250m

500m

Langstrath Beck

▲ Sergeant's
Crag

Stockley
Bridge

Glaramara
783m

Stonethwaite Fell

▲ Green Gable
801m

750m

Great Gable
899m

750m

Styhead
Tarn

Seathwaite
Fell

Climber's
Traverse

Sprinkling
Tarn

500m

Allen
Crags
785m

Langstrath Beck

500m

750m

500m

Round
How

750m

Angle Tarn

Ill Crags

Scafell Pike
978m

N

0   3 Kilometres

0   2 Miles

WALK 24: The Traverse of Scafell Pike

Map: The main part of the walk, from Stockley Bridge, is on the English Lakes SW sheet, from Seathwaite to Stockley Bridge is on the NW sheet (1:25,000).
Start: MR235122. Seathwaite. Park on the verge before the farm.
Distance: 9 miles (14km)
Time: 6hrs.
What's it Like?: A magnificent high mountain traverse. The ambience is entirely rocky from beginning to end—no pastoral relief on this walk, no sylvan bowers. Rugged and rough, but except in a few places the going is not too bad. Crags abound, big and small, and some savage gills too, so this is not a walk for bad weather. In such conditions navigational competence of a high order is required. Quite tiring—there's about 3000ft (900km) of ascent involved.
Links with Other Walks: (1) Instead of Grains Gill an approach can be made by the Glaramara–Allen Crags ridge—the first part of Walk 25; (2) The route can be joined to Walk 14, The Crinkle Crags-Bowfell ridge, starting and ending in Langdale. A very long, hard day—about 13 miles (21km).
Shorter Alternatives: Follow the Grains Gill path to the top of Ruddy Gill then follow the broad path north-west past Sprinkling Tarn to Sty Head. Descend either via the main Sty Head path or the Taylor Gill path. 5 miles (8km), 1600ft (488m) of ascent.
Bad Weather Alternatives: Borrowdale has numerous short walks suitable for breaks in the weather, especially by the riverside between Rosthwaite and Grange. Or one could visit Watendlath and the Bowder Stone. Ultimately, there are the bright lights of Keswick.

Above: **Sprinkling Tarn from Scafell Pike.**

A Walk Across the Roof of England

At 3209ft (978m) Scafell Pike is the highest summit in England. It lies at the very heart of the western fells and because of this is readily

Above: **Great End seen from Grains Gill**.

Above right: **The path crosses the top of Pier's Gill**.

climbed from any of several valleys: Wasdale, Langdale, Borrowdale or Eskdale. Each route is different and has its merits, but that from Borrowdale is perhaps best of all because it can be turned into a natural traverse which reveals more of the mountain and its surroundings than any other. There are in fact three peaks to cross, for Ill Crag and Broad Crag are quite distinctive entities even though linked to the main summit. Perhaps one should speak of the Scafell Pikes—in the plural—despite the Ordnance Survey.

The walk starts and ends in the hamlet of Seathwaite, at the very head of Borrowdale, and the wettest inhabited place in the country. Just before the farm buildings there is parking space on the left hand grass verge which though normally adequate can quickly fill on a warm summer's day. It is the early bird which catches the parking space at Seathwaite! The alternative is the car park at Seatoller, a mile down the valley, which is also the starting point for those coming by bus from Keswick. At the end of the day it can seem a very long mile!

There are other reasons too why an early start is advisable: this is a long, high walk across very rough terrain and you should have time in hand to deal with tiredness or emergencies. In bad weather it is the preserve of the experienced fellwalker and competent navigator.

From the hamlet a broad path leads along the river to Stockley Bridge. Time is healing the land a little now, but there is still enough evidence around to tell of the devastating floods of 1966 which hit Borrowdale like a tidal wave. Considerable embankment work has been done to try and contain the river and so far it seems to have worked.

Stockley Bridge will be our point of return for beyond the bridge the path diverges; that on the left is our outward path via Grains Gill and that on the right our homeward path from Sty Head. The path climbs the gill which higher up becomes Ruddy Gill, crossed by a footbridge. Higher still, as the great bulk of the Great End crags appear over the lip of the land, the gill becomes something of a ravine and shows how it got its name from the tell-tale traces of haematite. By the time the path has finished playing tag with the gill, Great End towers up at the head of its scree slopes. The big gullies look deep and sinister except in winter when Great End assumes a truly alpine appearance and the gullies make superb ice climbs. Great End shares with Helvellyn the distinction of having the most consistently

Above: **Sty Head Tarn is one of the most popular places in the Lake District.** (Photo: Duncan Unsworth).

Facing page, top: **The Scafell massif seen from Kirk Fell. The traverse described more or less follows the skyline left to right to the deep notch of Mickledore. The Corridor Route follows a line above the lower crags.** (Photo: Duncan Unsworth).

Facing page, bottom: **Wastwater from Scafell Pike.** (Photo: Duncan Unsworth).

good winter climbing conditions in the district.

Allen Crags and Esk Pike form the foreground as the path traverses towards Esk Hause, the hub of the great wheel of fells. From the far side of the Hause, upper Eskdale stretches away, sombrely bleak; the most primeval-looking landscape in the district.

From the Hause a line of cairns leads into Calf Cove, climbing gently then more steeply up a rough scree slope. Ill Crag dominates the scene ahead—a typical 'trick' summit that looks like your final goal until you actually get there and discover the awful truth that there is still some way to go! This is the sort of summit that gets fellwalking a bad name because it discourages children and sometimes their parents, too. However, Ill Crag *is* a summit—at 3068ft (935m) it is just a metre higher than the adjacent Broad Crag and so the second highest of the Pikes.

Before Ill Crag can be reached, however, the path crosses a stretch of large stones which slow down progress and beyond which the real summit of the mountain comes into view, discouragingly. The angle of the climb eases in compensation and the big blocks give way to gravel which is easier on the feet. It is a simple matter now to make a small diversion from the main path and climb Ill Crag.

Now the path descends to a col before climbing steeply up the rough slopes of Broad Crag. The ground is covered with a variety of stone blocks reminiscent of the worst parts of Wasdale Screes and the path, if it can be so called, would need all the skills of an Indian scout to find were it not for the line of marking cairns. It takes a real effort of willpower to leave the path and climb to the summit of Broad Crag (3064ft/934m).

Beyond Broad Crag there is a narrow col and then the final climb, still on rough blocks, to the summit plateau of Scafell Pike where there is a huge cairn (3209ft/978m). Climb up the cairn and you are, for a moment, the highest person in England, with a view that stretches from the Isle of Man to the Pennines.

There is a way down to the Lingmell Col direct from the summit, but it is scenically more rewarding to continue across the mountain top to the deep gap before Scafell known as Mickledore. Here the fellwalker can be forgiven for thinking he is at the limit of his powers, for great rocks shoot up all round and the col that is Mickledore itself seems small and insecure. The gap in the rocks that appears as though it might lead to the top of Scafell is the way of the notorious Broad Stand and not for humble fellwalkers like ourselves. Unfortunately, the difficulties are short enough to tempt and tricky enough to kill.

On the right of Mickledore and beyond it lies the vast face of Scafell Crag, the mightiest in Lakeland. It is an awesome sight. Different perspectives, each as impressive as the last, can be got by continuing the walk down a steepish scree gully from Mickledore to below Pikes Crag and looking back at the face from time to time. Pikes Crag itself gives what is probably the best viewpoint of all, but alas, is a fairly stiff scramble even on its shortest side and genuine rock-climbing everywhere else.

A path traverses below the fluted rocks of Pikes Crag and joins the main path climbing to Lingmell Col. From here the way ahead is known as the Corridor Route, and is one of the most magnificent high-level footpaths in the Lake District. A series of grassy shelves stretches towards Sty Head, with crags and broken ground above and below and the footpath traces a gradually descending line across this. The views across to Gable and the Pillar group are never less than grand, but it is the closer vignettes, such as the startling view down Piers Gill, a savage gully, which stay in the memory.

Eventually, at the top of Great End, the Corridor Route joins the path from Sprinkling Tarn to Sty Head. There is no need to continue to Sty Head itself, for a path cuts across towards the tarn and joins the main descent path. This crosses the stream at a bridge and continues down, wide and repaired in parts, to Stockley Bridge, Seathwaite and the car.

101

WALK 22: Glaramara and Langstrath

Map: English Lakes 1:25,000. The start and finish of the walk are on the NW sheet, the rest on the SW sheet.
Start: MR251137. The cottages called Mountain View, on the Borrowdale road. Limited parking, but there is a good car park 5 minutes' walk away at Seatoller.
Distance: 10 miles (16km).
Time: 6$\frac{1}{2}$hrs.
What's it Like?: A classic ascent with a bit of scrambling at the end which can be avoided, followed by an easy ridge then a long, long, descent alongside one of Lakeland's finest becks. No technical difficulties at all, but a certain degree of stamina required.
Shorter Alternatives: (1) Ascent and descent the same way, 3$\frac{1}{2}$hrs; (2) At Allen Crags, instead of turning left to go down Langstrath, turn right and go down Grains Gill—saves at least an hour, probably more, and is a good walk in its own right; (3) A stroll up Langstrath from Stonethwaite (parking) to Tray Dub and back takes about 2$\frac{1}{2}$hrs—easy walking and delectable bathing on a hot day! (4) A stroll into the heart of Combe Gill and back takes about 1$\frac{1}{2}$hrs. Fine rock scenery.
Bad Weather Alternative: Retire to the wild fleshpots of Keswick.

Above: **Combe Head, Glaramara.**

A Lovely Fell and a Lost Valley

Glaramara commands the head of Borrowdale, thrusting out into the valley and exhibiting all the qualities of an important mountain. It queens it over this part of the dale, demanding attention, tempting walkers with the hidden recesses of Combe Gill and climbers with the crags which are there. In shape too it is undeniably attractive, and there is that romantic-sounding name—what more could a fell want? Not much apparently, for Glaramara is at one end of a short ridge, the other end of which is taken up by a fell called Allen

Right: **The path from Esk Hause to Langdale.**

Below:**Climbing Glaramara with Borrowdale behind.**

Crags, which is actually 7ft (2m) higher than Glaramara—but who has heard of Allen Crags?

The ascent is made from Mountain View Cottages on the Borrowdale road, about five minutes' walk from the car park at Seatoller. It follows an extremely attractive line up a long spur of fellside and is perhaps the most elegant ascent in Lakeland, though one hesitates to match it against say, the Hall's Fell ascent of Blencathra (See Walk 32). But it picks its way to the top with what old Omar Khayyam would call 'logic absolute' and is never unduly steep. The return by way of Langstrath is fairly lengthy—the valley certainly earns its name—but the beck is one of the finest in Lakeland and well worth the effort.

Opposite Mountain View Cottages there is a narrow road and the walk starts along this for a few yards before a stile on the left gives access to the main path into Combe Gill. This climbs up through some trees and breaks out onto the open fellside, all the time climbing gradually by the side of a beck. (It would seem logical that the beck is actually Combe Gill, and not the hollow, which according to the Ordnance Survey is simply called the Combe, but Combe Gill is the name invariably bestowed on both.) Just beyond an old sheep-fold the path veers away from the stream and starts to climb steadily up the lumpy ridge on the right.

It is truly a delightful ascent; never too steep, never too strenuous. There is even a little rock step to be negotiated, but nothing difficult, and if the views are at first a little confined, before long there's a marvellous view to be had down the length of Borrowdale. Gillercomb comes into view as well, and Honister Crag. On a clear day you can see right through to the coast and beyond it to the hills of Galloway. Nearer, the great Combe itself reveals its secrets. Tiers of crags rise up to buttress Glaramara and on the other flanks of the hollow there are endless outcrops. The large clean-looking outcrop directly across from our viewpoint is Doves' Nest, where a huge slice of rock has slipped down the mountain leaving a gap between the two which can be explored by those who feel intrepid enough. The caves require a torch and some scrambling skill, but rumour has it that there has been another rock fall recently, so it is perhaps better to keep away!

At the head of the combe is Raven Crag and on its left Combe Gill tumbles down from the curious notch called Combe Door. In a hard winter of good snow it is a splendid mountaineering expedition to climb up to the door, then over Combe Head and so to the summit.

Langdale Pikes from the Glaramara – Allen Crags Ridge. (Photo: Duncan Unsworth).

Langstrath. (Photo: Duncan Unsworth).

Where the angle of the ridge eases the ground becomes increasingly boggy and the path less distinct. The summit appears as a large rock mound across this morass with the subsidiary—but much more elegant—top of Combe Head on the left. The path is far from clear but there is a cairn here and there built, one feels, more in hope than expectation.

Eventually you fetch up at the foot of the summit buttress and a line of scratched rocks shows the way up. This is a nice little scramble (a frozen cascade of ice in winter) and though not difficult, anyone who wishes to avoid it can do so by a large detour round the rocks to the right. Either way, the top of the rocks is the summit of Glaramara (2569ft/783m).

The climb to the summit takes about two hours—the rest of this fairly lengthy expedition is taken up with the return!

A clear path runs along the hummocky ridge between Glaramara and Allen Crags. There are some boggy bits, but the compensation lies in the innumerable small tarns which cause the bog—they form beautiful foregrounds to the Langdale Pikes and Bowfell. In the right light, Flat Crags on Bowfell looks very striking from here. Over to the west the huge buttresses of Great End are particularly impressive, the gullies showing as black gashes in summer but white streaks in winter; one of the best winter climbing areas in the Lakes.

The ridge ends at Allen Crags (2576ft/ 785m), the highest point on the walk, but insignificant as a mountain. Immediately below is the cruciform drystone walling which forms a well-known windbreak and the rather bleak slopes swelling up to Esk Hause. This is the very heart of the Lake District; the hub of the wheel that Wordsworth imagined the valleys formed. And indeed you can sense it; everything is so near, Langdale, Eskdale, Borrowdale . . . There's many a weary fellwalker, caught in a winter blizzard, who has staggered down the wrong valley by mistake.

Our valley, Langstrath, is not so readily accessible, despite the fact that it lies right there at our feet as we walk down from Allen Crags to join the path from Esk Hause. It is true that the map shows a path gaily going down Allencrags Gill into the valley, but don't you believe it. There is no path and the way is an exceedingly steep boulder-strewn slope. The real way is to follow the broad path which leads towards Rossett Gill until the brooding waters of Angle Tarn are reached when there is a small path following the beck down into the valley.

The next mile and a half, traversing upper Langstrath, passes through some wild country. The place is a great sombre valley head, very boggy and with a path which plays hide and seek. First you see it, then you don't. All the guide books will tell you that there is a path on either side of the river, and so there is of sorts. The path on the other side always looks better—especially when you've just crossed over!

There are rock outcrops all along the valley, particularly on the Glaramara side, and some good scrambles exist up there for those who like the feel of rock. Down in the valley the Langstrath Beck, quite wide, splashes down over small cascades and through some deep pools, although as yet there is no real hint of the glories to come.

These begin at the bridge where the Stake Beck comes tumbling down to join the Langstrath. Joined now by the route from Stake Pass the path improves and crosses the main stream by a second bridge at a splendid waterfall and pool called Tray Dub. From here down, the beck is quite magnificent, with two more notable pools—Swan Dub and Blackmoss Pot—and many lesser ones. In a land of fine streams, this is one of the best.

On the east side of the valley Sergeant's Crag with its prominent gully rises on the skyline and ramparts of rock run along to the end of the valley where Eagle Crag forms a bold cornerstone. By this time the path has become a broad bridleway as it passes through woods and turns the corner into Stonethwaite valley. There's a variation here which takes you down by the stream and through the camp site, but Stonethwaite and the thought of a drink beckons, to help the last mile back to the car.

WALK 26: Great Gable and the Climbers' Traverse

Map: English Lakes (NW) 1:25,000.
Start: MR 235122. Seathwaite. There is parking just before the farm is reached.
Distance: 6 miles (10km).
Time: 5 hrs. Much of this route is time-consuming scrambling.
What's it Like?: An unusual expedition full of interest, excitement and good views. There's a lot of scrambling but nothing difficult or exposed—easier than Yewbarrow or Sharp Edge, for example. Good balance and mountain sense required or you could end up with a broken ankle, it's that sort of terrain. Quite tiring. Not a bad weather route. In winter it is a magnificent outing—for a trained mountaineer.
Shorter Alternatives: (1) Reverse the route described as far as Great Gable, descend Aaron Slack to Styhead Tarn and back by Taylorgill Force or Stockley Bridge—4 miles (6km), 3hrs; (2) Follow the route described as far as Sty Head then take the good path south to Sprinkling Tarn and descend Grains Gill back to

Seathwaite—5¹/₂ miles (9km), 3hrs.
Bad Weather Alternatives: Retire to the fleshpots of Keswick. These are the only fleshpots in the vicinity, so don't knock them.

Napes Needle and the World of the Rock-Climber

Of all the Lakeland fells Great Gable is the one held in most affection by walkers. Its sugar-loaf profile, its romantic-sounding name, its dominating position at the head of Wasdale and its fine crags have all contributed to what many regard as the ideal mountain. When the Fell and Rock Club, the senior mountaineering club of the district, decided on a memorial to members who had died in the 1914–18 war it was on Gable that they placed it not, as one might have expected, on Scafell Pike. The top of the peak and some adjacent fells were given to the National Trust in memory of the fallen

Above: **Great Gable and Sprinkling Tarn. The red screes of Great Hell Gate can be seen with the Napes on the left. The upper rocks are Westmorland Crags.**

Above left: **The hanging valley of Gillercombe, with Sour Milk Gill. The peak in the background is Grey Knotts, with the large crag of Gillercombe Buttress. The Upper Seathwaite Slabs can be seen at the top of the gill, near the path.**

Above right: **Nearing the end of the Climbers' Traverse, with the Sphinx Rock.**

and a memorial service is held on the summit on Remembrance Sunday; usually well attended. Long before that a profile of Napes Needle was adopted as a badge by the club.

The usual way to climb Gable is either from Sty Head by a very direct and worn path or more elegantly from Honister Hause across the tops of Grey Knotts, Brandreth and Green Gable, but there is a more exciting way and that is to follow the Gable Girdle, a succession of paths which leads around the fell just below the crags. Below the Napes Ridge the path was first made by rock-climbers to enable them to reach the crags and so it is often referred to as the Climbers' Traverse.

The ascent begins from Seathwaite, a cluster of farm buildings at the head of Borrowdale. There is an archway through the buildings on the right which leads to a walled lane running down to the river and a bridge. This is where we will return to at the end of the day, God willing, but for now we turn away from the steep and rocky path which climbs the fellside directly ahead and go up-river, at first along the banks of the Derwent then climbing steadily as path and river diverge until Taylorgill Force is reached. This is a splendid waterfall, long and narrow. The route up by the side of the fall is steep and scrambly and

not for the nervous, but nowadays this can be by-passed and the path followed without much bother until it is joined by the much more frequented path from Stockley Bridge.

The broad path runs on to the Styhead Tarn. This always seems a lost and lonely place despite the fact that the pass is one of the most frequented in the Lakes. Beyond the tarn a blue Mountain Rescue box marks the top of the pass and acts as a focus for the several routes which converge here.

The one we want slopes off up the fell until at a cairn it divides into two. The direct way to the summit lies with the path on the right but we want the one on the left, not quite so well worn, which climbs up to some large boulders below an impressive rock face called Kern Knotts. Kern Knotts is a short flat wall forming an angle with a more broken wall on the right. It is split by two very prominent cracks. That on the left is Kern Knotts Crack, quite wide, and the thinner one on the right is Innominate Crack. Kern Knotts Crack was first climbed by the great Owen Glynne Jones in 1897. It was regarded as a test piece for many years and though by modern climbing standards it is well down the scale of difficulty, it has become polished with use and is still by no means easy.

Our route now goes to the left below the rest of Kern Knotts Crag where the going can be difficult because of large boulders, but eventually it eases and leads out across a wide shoot of distinctly red-coloured scree, called Great Hell Gate. The rock scenery is already superb; Tophet Bastion rises directly ahead and the curious Hell Gate Pillar sticks out of the scree, high up the gully. Once across the gully we are in the region of the Great Napes.

The Great Napes consist of a fan-like series of ridges and gullies which build to an apex some 300ft (91m) above. Our path (or paths, for there's ribbon development going on here!) runs below these rocks, up and down like a bit of a switchback. The thing everyone looks for, of course, is the famous Napes Needle, expecting it to appear as it does in the well-known photographs, which show it as a sharp arrowhead etched against the sky. Unfortunately, from below it doesn't look like that and since it blends in with the rock behind, it can easily be missed. The real Arrowhead at the foot of the ridge of that name, or even the Cat Rock, are sometimes mistaken for the Needle.

Things are not helped by the path. The simplest traverse runs more or less level and well below the crags but soon after the Tophet rocks at the start of the Great Napes, a fair path climbs higher, so as to be right up against the rocks. Perhaps the easiest way to identify the Needle from below is to look out for Needle Gully, which is quite big, steep and distinctive. In fact it is the first big gully after Great Hell Gate.

Once at the gully there is no mistaking the Needle or the great ridge which rises from it. The best view, however, is obtained from a ledge admirably named the Dress Circle which is reached by a simple scramble after the gully. It is from here that the well-known pictures are taken.

Napes Needle really does live up to its name. It is very sharp indeed and I can assure you, as one who has been there, that when two or three are gathered together on the Needle tip, there's not much room for manoeuvre. It was first climbed by W.P. Haskett Smith, alone, in 1886, a feat which is regarded by many climbers as the start of rock-climbing as a sport.

The Dress Circle is below Eagle's Nest Ridge and if there are climbers on the route known as Eagle's Nest Direct then you get a good view of some acrobatic footwork. Acrobatic footwork is what you will next need yourself, though in a very minor key, for the ongoing route below the crags is scrambly and needs care, though

there is nothing difficult about it. The Arrowhead Ridge comes next and it is easy to see why it is so called, though the arrow lacks the separation from the main crag which is what makes Napes Needle so distinctive. Beyond Arrowhead is Cat Rock or the Sphinx—I prefer the latter name because the perched block really does seem like a smaller version of the Egyptian monument—and beyond that again the long scree shoot of Little Hell Gate.

You may well need to descend a bit before the scree, but it doesn't really matter so long as you follow a path below the broken rocks of the White Napes to the top of Gavel Neese, a steep grassy rib which plunges down into Wasdale Head. A clear path climbs this rib and

Above: **Wasdale Head from Great Gable.** (Photo: Duncan Unsworth).

Right: **Stockley Bridge.** (Photo: Duncan Unsworth).

extensive, ranging from Carrock Fell in the north to Black Combe in the south, but for the picturesque view it is usual to walk across the stony plateau towards Wasdale, where another cairn can be found built in 1876 by two brothers, Thomas and Edward Westmorland, to mark the viewpoint they considered was the best in the district. Certainly the view down Wasdale is very fine—but the best? The best views come from lower elevations than Great Gable and I would match the views from Loughrigg or Muncaster Fell against this one any day!

By returning from Westmorland Cairn to the summit a path can be found continuing in roughly the same direction, leading to Windy Gap, which is the deep notch between Great Gable and Green Gable. From here it is only a few minutes to the top of Green Gable (2628ft/801m). There is a fine view from here of Gable Crags, which always look sombre and are much more savage looking than the more famous Napes.

From the summit of Green Gable a cairned path leads into the head of Gillercomb, a broad hanging valley drained by Sour Milk Gill. It can be very boggy in this valley but the scenery is worth it—crags and outcrops range all round, especially the great bastion of Gillercomb Buttress, which is the rocky face of Grey Knotts. Under snow the valley is truly alpine in character, and I well remember an epic struggle I had one winter in Gillercomb Gully, with no ice axe, a big framed rucksack and hob-nailed boots. That was in the days of the DIY school of mountaineering, which was the best school of all—if you survived!

The valley gives a very gentle walk down until it tips over the edge into Borrowdale. At this point there are some large easy slabs by the stream known as the Upper Seathwaite Slabs which provide lots of scope for fun climbing and scrambling of the easier sort. Then the path and the stream meet at a wall and the stream suddenly becomes a plunging cascade, splashing and dashing down the rocky fellside.

The path follows it down; steep and scrambly. In dry weather Sour Milk Gill is not much to write home about, but after a period of persistent rain it can be thunderous, wild and exciting. At the bottom there's the Lower Seathwaite Slabs which are much more challenging than the upper ones; neat little practice climbs.

When the path reaches the bridge over the infant Derwent our circuit is complete. It only remains to walk through the arch and join the car.

runs along the side of the fell to Beck Head, which lies between Gable and Kirk Fell. This path is part of an ancient way known as Moses Trod, said to have been used by a legendary quarryman named Moses who distilled illicit whisky on the side. Whether Moses existed or not, the route was most likely a pack-horse track for transporting slate from the Honister Quarries to Ravenglass, probably across Burnmoor. As the col is reached the path climbs a bit. One branch leads off below the dark crags on this side known as Gable Crag and another climbs steeply up the side of Gable to the top (2950ft/899m).

At the summit cairn is the memorial tablet mentioned earlier. The view all round is

WALK 27: The Jaws of Borrowdale

Map: English Lakes (NW) 1:25,000.
Start: Grange in Borrowdale, at the bridge.
Distance: 5¹/2 miles (9km). Circular.
Time: 2¹/2 hrs.
What's it Like?: This is a most beautiful valley walk. There is a good, clear path the whole way and the going is easy throughout. Moreover there are two villages en route, as well as Grange, where refreshment can be had.
Shorter Alternatives: Various tracks descend the fellside towards the New Bridge and Rosthwaite and any of these can be used to shorten the walk. Not as fine.
Bad Weather Alternatives: This walk is quite safe in all weather conditions, and the only alternative to remaining in Keswick is to undertake the outing of Walk 28.

Woods, River and Rock

The view from Friar's Crag across Derwent Water and into the mouth of Borrowdale was described by John Ruskin as one of the three finest in Europe. The broad lake stretches across the immediate horizon, dotted with wooded islands and flanked by crags which are themselves half hidden by trees as in a painting by Claude. Beyond the far end of the lake the valley perceptibly narrows and is further blocked by a wooded pinnacle, in what is known as the Jaws of Borrowdale. It is a scene which is never less than beautiful and in certain light, when a slight heat haze plays over the water, it can assume an almost magical quality. The Romantic movement of the late eighteenth century needed to look no further than this to find their ideal landscape.

Borrowdale starts at the end of the lake with the broad, green, flood-plains of the Derwent River; as clear a river as you are ever likely to find in these islands of ours. Clean round pebbles form the bed and sometimes the banks too, especially at low water.

Above: **The path climbs up past Castle Crag and gives a fine view back to Derwentwater and Skiddaw in the distance.**

Above left: **Rosthwaite in Borrowdale and the Stonethwaite valley with Greenup Edge.**

Above right: **The famous double-arched bridge at Grange in Borrowdale.**

Beyond the flood-plain, at the entrance to the Jaws, lies the hamlet of Grange, so called because it was a grange of Furness Abbey in the old days. It is an attractive, much photographed village, chiefly because of its double-arched bridge over the river, which looks almost Italianate, as though transported from the sun-drenched Appenines. Our walk starts here.

A narrow walled road leads out of the centre of Grange towards Hollows Farm and the upper valley. On the right the mountain wall seems steep, close and threatening, but across the narrow vale sunlight dapples the woods and at the turn of summer especially, the scene is idyllic. It's all Claude again; soft grey crags brushed by the massed browns, golds and greens of autumn.

The lane turns up towards Hollows Farm but a broad path carries on straight ahead, past a camp site and down to a lovely bend in the river at Dalt Wood. Pendulous branches overhang the water and in the distance can be seen Bowder Crag poking out of the trees. A beck empties itself into the river, ribbon-like, shallow, and the path divides. On the left is the way we shall return but on the right a good path climbs steadily uphill, bursting out of the trees and heading for a narrow col.

On the right is Lobstone Band, the main fellside, and on the left is the great tooth which sticks out of the Jaws, Castle Crag. It really is craggy, too, with some mostly forgotten rock-climbs, caves and memories of old Milli-can Dalton, a sort of pre-war hippy in the days before such people existed. Dalton spent his summers camping in the caves and to his disciples he was a sort of latter-day messiah. Others were less enthusiastic; when I asked a famous pre-war climber about him, he dismissed him as a dirty old man!

Our walk goes past Castle Crag, but it is easy to climb it by the obvious stony path in about fifteen minutes. It was the site of a Romano-British fort, and some ditches remain.

Once at the col the path levels out and you can look back down Broadslack Gill, which you have just climbed, to see Derwent Water and Skiddaw framed between the mountains. The walking is easy, along a broad path which I was brought up to call the Old Toll Road, though this name really only applies to the road built from Honister Quarries to Seatoller, which connects with our path. The old maps make it plain that the real road ran along the other side of the valley as it does today.

In autumn the whole of this fellside burns

111

with golden bracken. The trees are absent now from the immediate vicinity. Instead, the clear slopes, called Lingy Bank, run sweeping down to the valley floor and the hamlet of Rosthwaite. This sudden opening out of the vista is a revelation. You are surprisingly high up the fellside—or at least, so it seems, though in truth you are only some 400ft (120m) above the village—and this gives a grandstand view of the valley. Directly in front, funnelling away to the south-east, is the side valley at Stonethwaite with the thrusting bastion of Eagle Crag giving it distinctive form. Over there, by Greenup Edge, lies the way to Grasmere—and a grand walk it is too. Perhaps more than anything else, Glaramara attracts the eye, even though it is not a showy fell in the way that Great Gable or Pavey Ark are.

Glaramara is Borrowdale's finest offering in the way of high mountains. In fact, as this walk continues you might come to the justifiable conclusion that Borrowdale is not the place to look for high mountains. If that is your forte, then you'd be better off in Langdale or Wasdale. Of course, Borrowdale is a way *into* the high fells, but it is not *of* them. Borrowdale is all about rocks and trees and the river.

Beyond Scaleclose Gill another col is reached and shortly after that the main track joins the Old Toll Road down Honister. Our way lies steeply down to the left, into the hamlet of Seatoller, a cluster of old stone cottages at the foot of Honister Hause, one of the best-known passes in the Lake District. The road over the pass has been surfaced within living memory. The Honister Slate Company built the Old Toll Road at the end of the last century, but some years later there was a terrible accident when a motor truck carrying workmen down to Seatoller overturned on the rough road. According to the Seatoller woman who told me this tale, a number of workmen were killed and the road was surfaced soon after.

From the car park at Seatoller the way leads through Johnny Wood to Longthwaite. The wood belongs to the National Trust and is an oak wood rich in ferns, designated an Area of Special Scientific Interest (ASSI). By taking the lower of the two possible paths the way goes past the delightful Folly Bridge and the ruins of the Hoggart—once the object of interest to a climbing club I belonged to who wished to convert the hut for the use of club members. Planning consent was denied, as it usually is for any development outwith the confines of the villages.

The path continues by wood and stream to

the bridge at Longthwaite and then across this and through the fields to Rosthwaite, another stone-built village of attractive nooks and crannies. Our way does not actually penetrate into the commercial centre of this metropolis (post office cum shop and pub) but turns towards the river again, along a broad well-constructed path which leads to the New Bridge. I remember coming down off the fells once before the New Bridge was built, when the only way across the river was by stepping stones. Unfortunately it had been raining for about a week. The stepping stones had disappeared and my wife and I faced a broad, swift-flowing flood, cutting us off from Rosthwaite. Foolishly we stepped into the torrent. In no time the water was up to our waists and the current all but swept us off our feet. We were very thankful to reach the opposite bank in safety, I can tell you!

From the bridge the path follows the stream for half a mile or so, then climbs up through the woods, below Castle Crag until once again it comes down to the foot of Broadslack Gill. This was the way we set out, and all that remains is to follow the broad path and then the lane back to Grange.

The Jaws of Borrowdale with Castle Crag standing sentinel. (Photo: Duncan Unsworth).

WALK 28: Watendlath and the Bowderstone

Above: **The path down the delectable Watendlath Valley.**

Map: English Lakes (NW) 1:25,000.
Start: MR254168. Bowderstone car park in Borrowdale.
Distance: 5 miles (8km). Circular.
Time: 3hrs.
What's it Like?: A delightful afternoon's walk along unmistakable paths, with no technical difficulty of any sort. Great views, showing Borrowdale at its best.
Shorter Alternatives: Park in Rosthwaite and walk over to Watendlath, returning the same way. 1¹/₂hrs including a cup of tea!
Bad Weather Alternatives: (1) Drive to Watendlath; (2) Stay at home and read the Herries novels.

Two Beauty Spots Joined by a Quiet Walk

The eastern side of the Jaws of Borrowdale rise from the valley floor in richly wooded tiers of crags. The crags extend further than this, up and down the vale, but they do seem more concentrated at this place where the valley narrows. There are all sorts of curiosities hidden in these woods and rocks, and various paths wandering in, out and about them. It isn't really *walking* country—more your poking about country, if you know what I mean. Nevertheless, the walk described in this chapter is quite enchanting and though short it does include two of the best-known sights of the Lake District.

There's a bit of roadside walking which can't be avoided, but a path keeps you separate from the traffic, and in any case even the road in this delectable valley is a beautiful journey. Also the walk is a bit steep going up to Watendlath and very steep coming down High Lodore, but the distance is only half a mile or so in each case, so that's all right.

Derwent Water. (Photo: Duncan Unsworth).

The walk begins in the National Trust car park near the old Quayfoot Quarry where in summer there's often a van selling excellent ice cream of the old-fashioned sort. From the car park the way goes immediately up the broad path from the roadside, past the chaotic jumble of slate boulders which now more or less fills Quayfoot Quarry. Not many years ago the quarry was an impressive hole with steep walls, then suddenly the whole thing collapsed—it must have made one helluva bang and I hope there were no nervous fellwalkers passing at the time!

The path continues up to the Bowderstone in a few minutes, passing on the way the 100ft (30m) slab of Woden's Face which, back in the 1960s, seemed to be perpetually festooned with ropes because it was a favourite practice ground for rock-climbers. The rock got very polished I remember and there was a heated scene one day when an over-ambitious father tried to drag his young son up it. The boy can't have been more than six or seven and couldn't reach the polished holds. The ensuing pantomime effectively blocked off the crag to other climbers who were somewhat irate. Sadly, the boy and his father disappeared whilst attempting the Matterhorn shortly after. *Sic transit gloria mundi.*

People still climb on Woden's Face, but the rock doesn't seem as careworn these days. Perhaps the tyros have gone elsewhere; a gymnasium climbing wall, no doubt.

Ironically, the real experts now tackle—the Bowderstone, would you believe? At least, this great lump of fallen stone has all sorts of 'routes' catalogued on it, though I've never actually seen anyone trying them. Most of them are hard gymnastic exercises, which is what modern rock-climbing is all about. Nothing to do with mountaineering.

Whether the Bowderstone fell from the crags above in some distant century or was dumped where it lies by a melting glacier even longer ago is a moot point I'm not prepared to argue. It is best regarded as a Victorian curiosity, 36ft (11m) high and weighing, so they say, 1970 tons. A substantial ladder leads to the top of the block which is surprisingly narrow and very slippery, having been polished by a million feet. As Mallory said of Everest the Bowderstone is climbed because it is there; there is no view worth mentioning from the top.

A track leads past Bowderstone Cottage back to the road and a little way further there is a lay-by with a gate and a National Trust notice 'Grange Fell'. From here a path climbs

Watendlath. (Photo: Duncan Unsworth).

quite steeply at first through Frith Wood until it emerges at the top edge of the wood and crosses the flanks of Brund Fell. As height is gained there are increasingly wide views of upper Borrowdale, looking down on Rosthwaite with a bird's eye and taking in the two arms of the valley and the grand fell of Glaramara.

This is a quiet track, but at a gate it leads onto one of the major paths of the Lake District; the way from Rosthwaite to Watendlath, broad, scarred and battered. It is surprising in a way that this path is so popular because though it leads to one of the most attractive hamlets in the district, it is very steep and tourists who come this way to Watendlath earn their views the hard way. No doubt they feel better for it.

Coming our way we've avoided the worst of it, but there is still some climbing to do before the path levels out (or at least it *seems* level after what has gone before). Gradually the crest of the ridge is attained and Watendlath lies below.

It really is one of the prettiest views imaginable; the tarn, the whitewashed cottages, the fringe of trees and the background of high fells. Like Tarn Hows (Walk 17) it has appeared on countless calendars and greetings cards.

The path leads down to it swift as an arrow, broad and well repaired in a sympathetic manner. Over the bridge there is a cottage selling teas and ice cream and surprisingly, there's a large car park too, for Watendlath is connected by road to Borrowdale at Barrow Bay.

Also surprising to anyone not in the know is the selection of paperback novels by Hugh Walpole which the tea shop sells, but this is because Watendlath was the home of Judith Paris, Walpole's most tempestuous heroine and, along with Rogue Herries (who lived at Rosthwaite), his most memorable character. The four books of the Herries Chronicles— *Rogue Herries, Judith Paris, The Fortress* and *Vanessa*—were written between 1929 and 1932. Set in Borrowdale and the northern Lakes they were immensely popular, as is witnessed by the fact that when Harold Macmillan republished them in omnibus form in 1939, 60,000 copies— at eight shillings and sixpence—were sold before publication.

They have never been out of print since, but does anyone really read Walpole today? He seems to belong to a happy time when regional novelists were much more in vogue. Perhaps today's readers are too sophisticated. The

regional novelists one best remembers are those whose work transcends the region, like the Brontës and Hardy.

Walpole lived in Borrowdale himself and he once had to settle a dispute over which house in Watendlath Judith Paris lived in. He pointed out that she was a totally fictional character and so could hardly have lived in any, but for all that one of the cottages still carries a sign 'The Home of Judith Paris'.

The majority of visitors to Watendlath either walk back to Rosthwaite, whence they came, or have somebody meet them by car—a useful ploy on a wet day, when the walk over from Rosthwaite can be used to fill in the odd hour or so. Our plan is altogether more noble, for we shall walk down the vale of Watendlath, below the eastern slopes of Grange Fell along a splendid path which epitomises the best of Lakeland. On the right, across the vale, are the frowning bastions of Reecastle Crags, another playground for the modern gymnastic climbers. By this time the path and Watendlath Beck come close together, the one complementing the other.

In about a mile we come to the edge of the woods and our path turns left to plunge down through the trees towards a sharp double bend in the stream where the water starts to cascade on its way to the famous Lodore Falls. The falls wouldn't have been famous at all if it wasn't for Southey with his childrens' poem about how the water comes down splashing, dashing, crashing and bashing—or words to that effect. All nonsense. It has to be very wet weather indeed before the falls at Lodore get anywhere near to dashing or crashing. Usually they are a tame series of cascades and the story is told of the man who enquired of their whereabouts only to be told he was sitting on them!

The path turns away from the stream for the last time and descends with increasing steepness towards Borrowdale. Shepherd's Crag lies on the right, but from this angle you cannot see the steep cliffs which make it one of the most popular climbing crags in Britain for the climber of average ability. Below lies the Borrowdale Hotel and the path pops out between the hotel and farm, onto the main road.

It only remains to walk the mile or so back to the car park and the ice cream van.

Above left: **The Bowder Stone.**

Above right: **The Lodore Beck above the falls.**

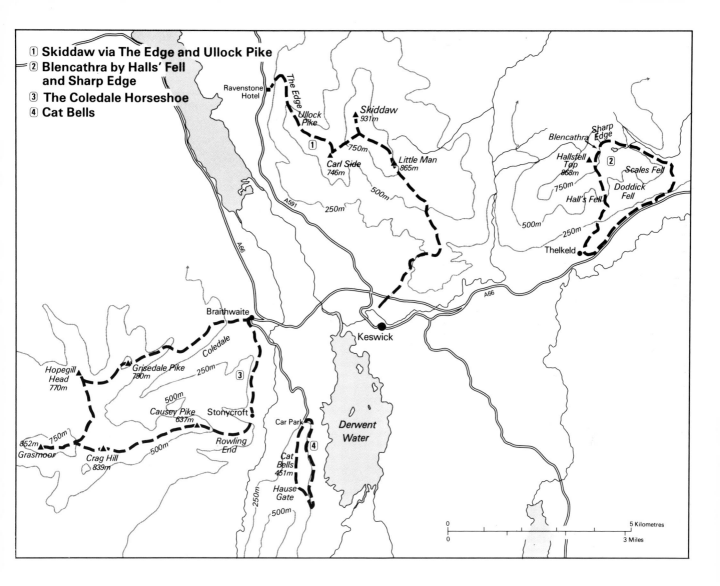

1. **Skiddaw via The Edge and Ullock Pike**
2. **Blencathra by Halls' Fell and Sharp Edge**
3. **The Coledale Horseshoe**
4. **Cat Bells**

Ravenstone Hotel

The Edge

Ullock Pike

Skiddaw
931m

① 750m

Carl Side
746m

Little Man
865m

500m

250m

A591

A66

Blencathra

Sharp Edge

Hallsfell Top
868m

② 750m

Scales Fell

Hall's Fell

Doddick Fell

500m

250m

Thelkeld

A66

Keswick

Braithwaite

Coledale

Grisedale Pike
790m

250m

Hopegill Head
770m

③

500m

Causey Pike
637m

Stonycroft

852m
Grasmoor

750m

Crag Hill
839m

500m

Rowling End

250m

Car Park

④

Cat Bells
451m

Hause Gate

500m

Derwent Water

0   5 Kilometres

0   3 Miles

WALK 29: Cat Bells

Keswick's Little Ridge

Cat Bells—the name means 'home of the wild cat'—is the first part of the distinctive ridge which extends along the west shore of Derwent Water. The ridge goes on to higher things—Maiden Moor and High Spy—and will take you all the way to Honister should you so wish, but in truth the first bit is the best and since it is a distinctive peak, can be regarded as a worthwhile outing in itself.

Because it is so very accessible (you could walk there from Keswick if you'd a mind to) and not very high (1480ft/451m), it is extremely popular. All sorts of people climb Cat Bells, and why not? For many it is their first climb, for some their first and last climb, the spirit of the hills having completely escaped them. It is certainly an excellent introduction for children since it is short, fairly sharp (it actually looks like a mountain, which is an

Above: **The view from Cat Bells – cloud caps the summit of Skiddaw.** (Photo: Duncan Unsworth).

118

Right: **Skelgill Bank, the start of the Cat Bells ridge.** (Photo: Duncan Unsworth).

Below: **Skelgill Bank from Cat Bells.** (Photo: Duncan Unsworth).

important consideration with youngsters) and the views are good. You can climb it on a lazy afternoon and still have time to stand and stare.

The walk begins at the north toe of the ridge where there is a car park (two in fact) although a more romantic approach is by motor launch from Keswick. The launches run regularly throughout the summer and you can land at Hawes End, just a few minutes from the start of the climb. A few yards from the car park a signpost which simply says 'path' points uphill and this is the way to go.

A good track zig zags up the fell which is very steep hereabouts, passing on the way a memorial tablet to Thomas Arthur Leonard, a nonconformist minister from Lancashire who was the founder of the Co-operative Holidays Association in 1892 and later the Holiday Fellowship; amongst the earliest of the 'out-door movements'. It reaches a first summit and the going is easier for a bit. On the left are some rock cuttings which are workings of the old Brandley Mine. The Brandley or Brandle-how Mine is scattered round the fellside between the ridge and the lake and was once one of the largest mines in the area, producing 300 tons of lead ore each year, and employing 70 or 80 men and boys. It is of considerable antiquity, unlike the Yewthwaite Mine on the other side of Cat Bells which probably wasn't worked until the late eighteenth century, but whereas the latter was a great success, the Brandley Mine was always plagued by flooding and seldom paid its way. Like most abandoned mine shafts, those on Cat Bells are dangerous and should not be investigated out of idle curiosity.

The ridge rises steeply to the final summit. There are fine views all round to the distant fells and also, aerial-like, down to Little Town in Newlands and the lake of Derwent Water.

Beyond the summit the path descends to a depression in the ridge known as Hause Gate, which is Old Norse for 'the pass road' and indicates it must have been a way across the ridge from Newlands to Borrowdale for a long time. There's a good path still, and we take it down towards Derwent Water, steeply zig zagging at first but then easing off until it is possible to join the Old Toll Road. During the descent there are fine views of the lake and the woods—the latter being the first purchase made in the Lake District by the National Trust in 1902.

Perhaps one of the best views of the lake is from the memorial seat to Sir Hugh Walpole which is just a short distance along the path above the woods. In 1923 Walpole bought Brackenburn, the large house which can be seen by the road below the path, and he died there in 1941. His affection for Borrowdale inspired his famous Herries Chronicles (see Walk 28).

The path touches the road at a small quarry but almost immediately leaves it again, climbing the fellside in a long slope before finally meeting the road again just a few yards from the car park.

Above: **Climbing the Cat Bells ridge.** (Photo: Duncan Unsworth).

Below: **Derwentwater and Cat Bells.**

WALK 30: The Coledale Horseshoe

Above: **Descending Grisedale Pike. Across the Vale of Keswick can be seen Skiddaw and Blencathra.** (Photo: Duncan Unsworth).

Map: English Lakes (NW) 1:25,000.
Start: MR233222. A lay-by just north of Stonycroft.
Distance: 11 miles (18km), including Grasmoor but not Whiteside.
Time: 7hrs.
What's it Like?: Arguably the best combination of linked ridges in the Lake District, with some unusual summits. Steep short pulls punctuate the ridges, which, for all that, have a certain smoothness about them. What a pity they are Skiddaw slates, and not Borrowdale volcanics!
Shorter Alternatives: (1) Climb Causey Pike only and return via Stonycroft Gill along an old mine track, 3hrs; (2) Climb Grisedale Pike direct from Braithwaite and return via Coledale, 4hrs.
Bad Weather Alternatives: Retire gracefully to Keswick, possibly via the well-known hostelry at Swinside.

Around the Valley of the Coledale Beck

In the north-west of the Lake District there is a final group of high fells lying between Crummock Water and the Vale of Newlands, which is as compact and self-contained as any in the district. Reduced to its simplest expression it consists of two ridges running parallel, east to west, joined at roughly their mid-point by a cross piece, so that the effect is of a letter H lying on its side. The bottom leg of the lazy-H consists of Causey Pike, Sail, Crag Hill and Grasmoor; the top leg is Whiteside, Hopegill Head, Sand Hill and Grisedale Pike, and the linking bit is Coledale Hause; a col between Coledale in the east and Gasgale in the west.

This formation is made the basis of a famous walk around the rim of Coledale, though Grasmoor, being the highest of the fells, is usually included for good measure. Apart from the start and the finish these are high-stepping ridges where a walker can stride out boldly, lapping up the miles.

Transport arrangements are a little awkward for this walk and ideally one should be dropped off at the roadside near Stair in the morning and picked up in the pub at Braithwaite at the end of the day, but if this is not practicable then resort must be made to a small lay-by on the narrow road which runs along the foot of the mountains, just north of Stonycroft. It is handy for the start, though less so for the finish, but one can't have everything.

From Stonycroft Gill a good path leads up through the bracken and heather of the well-shaped ridge to Sleet Hause, steep at first but then more gradual towards the rocky face of Causey Pike. What an old show-off this pinnacle is! If Skiddaw is Keswick's Mont Blanc, then surely Causey Pike is the town's Matterhorn. Like the real Matterhorn, it can be recognized at once from almost any angle; an identifying beacon in a sea of otherwise unrecognizable fells.

Yet it is a good little climb, needing a bit of scrambling to reach the summit, though the holds are as big as buckets and there isn't the least danger to life and limb. At the top you are likely to be met by predatory sheep, cadging goodies from passing humans. They are probably the only sheep in the world raised on Mars Bars.

Causey Pike is 2090ft (637m) and though from below it looks like a separate peak it turns out to be simply an incident on a long hummocky ridge which is followed westwards, first over Scar Crags then down to Sail Hause and steeply up the broad ruddy tinted path which climbs the flanks of Sail (2536ft/773m).

Sail is a good place from which to observe the desolate head of Coledale, made more sombre by the relics of the mining field. The Force Crag Mine on the far side of Coledale is easily seen and may or may not be working, depending on the vagaries of the industry, I suppose. The well-made broad tracks which penetrate some of the valleys like Coledale hereabouts, and seeming to go nowhere, once served mines which no longer exist.

The head of the valley at Coledale is most curious because it is in two tiers or broad steps, each guarded by a line of crags and each with its waterfall—High Force and Low Force respectively. It is a savage place and the mines give it a Wild West air so one feels it ought to be called Coledale Gulch and have a few cacti scattered about.

From Sail a magnificent little ridge, full of rock outcrops and narrow, connects with Crag Hill. The path teeters along the ridge then scrambles up amongst steep fellside and rocks to the barren plateau of the summit (2753ft/ 839m). For some time this fell was known as Eel Crag; a name now relegated to the rocks of the north face, overlooking Coledale Head. It is the very heart of this group of fells—the pivot around which they all turn, and so of some significance.

Beyond Crag Hill is a shallow depression separating it from Grasmoor. No narrow ridge this, but a broad hollow followed by a steady climb up to a plateau. The top is like something out of Conan Doyle's *Lost World;* an elevated plain hung in the sky and surrounded on all sides by extremely steep slopes. Professor Challenger would recognize the place at once, though it is a long time since prehistoric animals roamed there! The summit would be indistinguishable from the rest of the plateau were it not for an elaborate cairn, compartmentalised like a ruined cottage and useful as a shelter for eating lunch in (2795ft/

The ascent of Causey Pike by Rowling End. (Photo: Duncan Unsworth).

Above: **Grasmoor from Crag Hill.**
(Photo: Duncan Unsworth).

Right: **Grisedale Pike from near Coledale Hause.** (Photo: Duncan Unsworth).

852m). The view from the plateau can only be described as widespread, since it stretches from Whitehaven to Wetherlam.

This ascent of Grasmoor is, literally, out on a limb from the line of our walk and we must now return to the hollow below Crag Hill, then turn north down a shallow depression to reach Coledale Hause on the other side of which grassy slopes lead up to Sand Hill and Hopegill Head (2526ft/770m). From this top, those with plenty of energy can race out along the narrow ridge to Whiteside and back again, an excursion of some two miles or more, before continuing with the horseshoe proper. It gains another peak and gives outstanding views of the coastal plain (should anyone wish to view the coastal plain) but it does add an hour or so to the game plan.

From Hopegill Head the path teeters along the edge of Hobcarton Crag, playing hide and seek with a broken stone wall. It descends to a col where the edge is firm enough and flat enough to allow you to peer over the crag at its immense shattered face of unstable slate and grass. If only Hobcarton was firm granite—what a climbing crag it would make!

From there the route climbs to a subsidiary summit then dips and loops up to the top of the last and possibly the finest summit of the entire round, Grisedale Pike (2595ft/791m). It is the steepness of the final ridges which makes Grisedale Pike such a notable peak and if one were to continue the alpine analogy begun earlier, if Skiddaw is Mont Blanc and Causey Pike the Matterhorn, then Grisedale Pike must surely be the Weisshorn of Keswick. Like the Weisshorn, it is a child's mountain; straight up and down in an almost perfect triangle.

From the summit a long ridge runs down towards Braithwaite with a path which is initially steep—and in wet weather slippery. It joins the Whinlatter Pass road at the edge of the village and from there there is a mile and a half walk back to the car by paths through Braithwaite Lodge to join the road half a mile before the lay-by.

Right: **Looking back along the heather covered ridge to Causey Pike. The ridge in the distance is Cat Bells.** (Photo: Duncan Unsworth).

WALK 31: Skiddaw via the Edge and Ullock Pike

Above: **Skiddaw from Bassenthwaite lake. The Ullock Pike ridge described in the text follows the left hand skyline.**

Map: The English Lakes (NW) 1:25,000.
Start: MR235296. Ravenstone Hotel.
Distance: 7¹/2 miles (12km) (to Keswick town centre).
Time: 4¹/2hrs.
What's it Like?: Much more of a mountain excursion than one generally feels in the Lakes in the sense that it is a broad sweeping traverse. It is the grand gesture to a grand mountain, and in many ways not unlike the traverse of one of the easier Alpine peaks, like the Alphubel or the Balmhorn—though one would not press the analogy too far.

Though Skiddaw is an easy peak it is also a big peak; do not neglect warm clothing.
Shorter Alternatives: (1) Climb Latrigg from Keswick. Reverse the last part of the walk described and ascend to the top of Latrigg by any of several paths—good views—2hrs; (2) Walks are available in Thornthwaite Forest. There is parking and a picnic site at MR235281. Mirehouse is only a few hundred yards from the car park, too, so it could be a combined visit if the house is open; (3) Between Millbeck and Applethwaite there is a short stroll known as the Applethwaite Terraces. Good views over Derwent Water. Takes half an hour or so.
Bad Weather Alternatives: (1) Mirehouse has many literary associations and is open certain days (MR233284); (2) Keswick is full of pubs, cafes and restaurants, not to mention shops of all sorts. There is the excellent Fitz Park Museum in Station Road and the old station is itself now a railway museum.

A Traverse over Keswick's Great Fell

Of all the Lakeland fells, the one which consistently gets the worst press is Skiddaw, that great bulging hulk of a mountain dominating Keswick. It is indeed a much-maligned fell, often described as a plum pudding by

those who wish to denigrate it—but plum pudding can be very tasty at times.

One can see what the critics are getting at, of course. Seen from the town, or indeed, climbed from the town, Skiddaw is something of a wearisome toil and boring with it. There's a lot of effort for little reward. Not for Skiddaw the rocky pinnacles you find on the Langdale Pikes, nor even the exciting corries such as are found on Blencathra next door, but just bald slopes of grass and scree which seem to go on forever.

There are several fells in the Lake District which are even more boring than Skiddaw—Loadpot Hill or High Raise, for example—but Skiddaw is so *big*. People expect more from it.

Well there is more, but it has to be won. There is a grand ridge walk taking in the outlying peaks of Ullock Pike and Carl Side. Unfortunately it is a linear walk starting some five miles out of Keswick and ending back in the town, so transport is needed to reach the start. There is a bus service.

The walk starts at the Ravenstone Hotel on the Bassenthwaite road, A591. On the right of the hotel there is a path which climbs steeply through the surrounding woods until at last it breaks out into the open. After a while it is joined by a grassy path which goes up to the ridge line known as the Edge.

From the Edge an entirely new concept of Skiddaw is formed. A broad dale, Southern-dale, separates the Edge from the steep slopes of the great fell. And great it is; powerful in presence, dominating the wild dale below. There are even a few crags. In winter the scene is positively alpine; reminiscent of the Bernese Oberland.

The path climbs the Edge towards the sharp cone of Ullock Pike which it reaches without bother. Ullock Pike actually has twin summits, neither of which the Ordnance Survey bothers to provide with a height but it seems to be about 2264ft (690m). From here there are superb views over Bassenthwaite Lake whilst the way ahead, along a narrow ridge, appears most inviting.

The continuation ridge is known as Long-side Edge. It is high enough and narrow enough to give a feeling of real airy ridge walking and yet it is not in the Striding Edge or Hall's Fell class, so there is no difficulty in striding out. Up and down like a switchback to the summit of the ridge which is also called Long Side (2408ft/734m).

Now the path continues to a col which is the head of Southerndale, but the mound rising on the right of the path is Carl Side (2448ft/746m) and it is worth climbing to its broad top to get a fine view over Keswick and Derwent Water. To the south, beyond the lake, a tumbled mass of distant blue fells can be seen, for this is the northern outpost of the district. Nearer to hand are Skiddaw and Skiddaw Little Man,

Skiddaw. (Photo: Duncan Unsworth).

brooding and monstrous.

There is a little tarn at the col and on the far side a long scree slope which has to be climbed to reach the south summit of Skiddaw and the broad track which leads to the summit itself, (3055ft/931m). The top is broad, stony, and uninspiring and the same can be said about the view. The most interesting aspect of the latter is the intriguing views over the strange fells known collectively as 'Back o' Skidda'. They look more like the Pennines than the Lakes and the walking has a Pennine feel about it too. They are unusual and not all that easy—the traverse from Skiddaw House over Great Calva to Carrock Fell gives a good taste of the region.

Skiddaw House can be seen at the foot of the fell, lonely and not a little eerie. For many years it was a shepherd's bothy but it was recently turned into a youth hostel. It certainly makes a hostel which is comparable in loneliness with Black Sail in Ennerdale. Unfortunately, at the time of writing there is a disagreement with the planning authority and the future of the hostel seems in doubt.

The return to the south summit and the descent by the 'ordinary route' to Keswick is almost like treading hallowed ground, for it was certainly one of the earliest—if not *the* earliest—of tourist ascents in the Lake District. To climb Skiddaw was the done thing in those early days and Peter Crosthwaite, an eighteenth-century Keswick entrepreneur, had a beacon erected on the summit about 1786.

As can well be imagined, there is no problem in path finding. A broad track descends from the south summit and passes through a wire fence. Most true fellwalkers, however, leave the path before this and make for the twin-headed peak of Little Man (2838ft/ 865m). The ground falls away sharply to the west where a glade runs down to the hamlet of Millbeck. To the south lies Derwent Water and the fells beyond—a reprise of the Carl Side view, but perhaps even finer. It is of course a grand sweep and like all grand sweeps it lacks the intimacy of the lesser viewpoint. Nevertheless, Skiddaw Little Man offers the panorama *par excellence*.

By continuing across Little Man the main path to Keswick can be rejoined. Lower down it steepens and passes a monument erected in 1891 to the Hawells, who were noted breeders of Herdwick sheep. It seems a curious place to put a monument, but there it is and it marks what is virtually the end of the Skiddaw descent. The path meets a surfaced road shortly after (Gale Road) and a weary walker can be picked up here by car if he's lucky—or maybe not so lucky, for the walk into town around the slopes of Latrigg is really quite superb. Looking back at Skiddaw from here is perhaps the best view of the old rascal, and a certain sneaking affection might even be felt.

WALK 32: Blencathra by Hall's Fell and Sharp Edge

Map: English Lakes (NE) 1:25,000.
Start: MR325261. Gategill.
Best Access: From Threlkeld village, 4 miles (6km) from Keswick on the A66. The village lies just off the main road on the north side. Park in village. Various paths lead to Gategill, 20 minutes' walk.
Distance: 4¹/2 miles (7km). Circular.
Time: 3hrs.
What's it Like?: One of the finest mountaineering expeditions in the Lake District. The route as described is suitable only for experienced walkers with a head for heights. Short and not particularly strenuous. In winter this expedition can be quite serious; ice axe and crampons recommended in hard snow conditions.
Bad Weather Alternatives: (1) Visit Keswick: shops, boating, mini-golf and the interesting Fitz Park Museum and Art Gallery (Station Road); (2) Castlerigg Stone Circle (291236), a very fine Neolithic circle of 48 stones in a superb setting, a mile or so east of Keswick; (3) Brougham Castle (539290), about a mile east of Penrith on the A66. Extensive romantic ruins. Pronounced *broom*—'tis he of the carriage; (4) Dalemain House (477270), home of the Hasells since 1665.

Above: **On Hall's Fell.**

Two Ridges and a Fine Traverse

Blencathra rises like an alpine wall above Threlkeld's vale, all ridges and deep hollows. It is seen to perfection from St John's in the Vale or the ancient standing stones at Castlerigg, and especially in winter, when the comparison with the Alps is reinforced as the prominent ridges glisten with new snow. There are three of them. From left to right, looking at the mountain, they are Gategill Fell, Hall's Fell and Doddick Fell. On either side of these the mountain falls away in gentler-looking slopes, though out of sight, beyond the right-hand skyline's fringe of crags, lies the sombre Scales

Above left: **Winter turns the traverse of Blencathra into a mountaineering expedition. Hall's Fell ridge stands out clearly in this picture.**

Above right: **The view from Hall's Fell down the long central fault of the Lake District.**

Tarn and the most dramatic ridge of all, Sharp Edge.

It's all frontal show. The other side of Blencathra is made up of unutterably boring slopes leading to the lonely becks and wild, unkempt fells known as the Back o' Skidda'. Still, one mustn't grumble at this—some mountains don't offer half as much. Combining the central ridge—Hall's Fell—with Sharp Edge, makes what I consider to be the best traverse of any peak in the Lake District. As far as the walker is concerned its only possible rival is Helvellyn by Striding Edge and Swirral Edge (see Walk 35).

In winter, with ice and snow about, this is not an expedition for the inexperienced. An axe and crampons are more than welcome and a rope might be useful on the bad step of Sharp Edge. Under such conditions it can be a truly memorable mountaineering day.

As in most cases where difficult terrain is encountered, so much depends on conditions. In summer rain, Sharp Edge can be slippery— the rock is Skiddaw slate—but on a nice dry day, when the sun is shining and all's right with the world, you'll probably wonder what all the fuss is about. A modicum of care and a head for heights is all that's needed in those conditions.

It is best to leave the car in Threlkeld, which has a good pub if little else, and cross the fields to the farm complex at Gategill, immediately below Hall's Fell. The old mine at Gategill was one of the most productive lead mines in the area and is of ancient origin, though, as usual with such mines, it was abandoned and re-opened several times in its long history. Probably its most productive period was 1881–1901, when about one hundred men and boys were employed there and ore worth £120,473 was raised. The mine worked intermittently during the present century and was only finally abandoned during the last war, though according to experts the ore is far from being exhausted.

Gategill is also the home of the Blencathra foxhounds. The Blencathra is a famous hunt whose territory is the northern Lakes, the same country hunted by the renowned John Peel of Caldbeck (See Walk 40). Foxhunting in the Lake District is done on foot and is by no means confined to the wealthier classes. The hounds can cover prodigious distances—the records tell of the Blencathra pack once chasing a large dog fox from Skiddaw out to Portinscale, along Borrowdale and over Sty Head where it escaped under cover of darkness. The hounds continued their search, however, and were discovered at Coniston next morning, have covered some fifty miles of very rough country. To follow a Lakeland pack you need to be very fit!

You need to be pretty fit for the next bit of walking too! The path goes up by the beck and

crosses it just above the weir. The steep swelling bosom of Hall's Fell lies immediately ahead and the path curls round the convex slope like a ribbon laid across an upturned pudding basin. These slopes are won by hard graft, but once above them the true nature of Hall's Fell is revealed as it gathers itself into a considerable ridge.

A trace of path avoids the crest of the ridge, mostly on the right, but it is more fun to stick to the rocky top as much as possible, using hands as well as feet, where prudence dictates! The drop, particularly to the right, is awesome whether you are on the path or the ridge and a little way along here is the first crux of a winter traverse—some delicate little steps across very steep snow slopes, where a slip could send you tobogganing 800ft (240m) into Doddick Gill. In summer, it's the sort of place you'd hardly even notice!

The ridge leads absolutely directly to the summit cairn. The Ordnance Survey insist on calling it Hallsfell Top (2772ft/845m) but nobody else does and we can do without another name because Blencathra already has two. Its other name is Saddleback, from the shape of the fell when seen from certain directions, like St. John's in the Vale. Until fairly recently this was the name in common use, but it's nice to see the ancient British name of Blencathra returning to favour instead. Blencathra means 'the hill of the devils'.

The view from the summit is unusual. Somebody once said that you can see more flat land from Blencathra than from any other summit in Lakeland, because of its position on the edge of things. Though this may be true it isn't the whole picture. To the immediate north the wild fells 'Back o' Skidda' tumble away towards Carlisle, whilst to the south the great geological trench which bisects the Lake District can be seen to perfection. This trench runs between Blencathra and Skiddaw, continues through St John's in the Vale, over Dunmail Raise, and along the vales of Grasmere and Rothay to Windermere. It is as if some giant had brought a cleaver down on the hills and left a deep gash.

From the summit the way forward is to follow the broad ridge north to Foule Crag and Sharp Edge. Scales Tarn lies below in its deepset hollow, ringed around with crags. In mist this is dangerous ground to wander about on—it needs careful work with the compass to hit off the ridge exactly. But in fine weather there's no problem, although it always seems to me further than I last remember it!

The start of the ridge is shaly and scrambly leading down quickly to the *mauvais pas,* where a couple of resolute moves are called for. All this needs treating with care and so does the rest of the ridge, for although it becomes much easier after the bad step, a sudden relaxation of tension can lead to a fatal relaxation of vigilance. There's an old mountaineering adage that accidents usually happen in the easy places.

At the bottom of the ridge, which ends suddenly, a path leads away down the narrow, steep-sided valley of the River Glenderamackin, rising at the end to a low col. It's a queer place, for the little valley seems blocked by a whalebacked hill called Souther Fell, and indeed, the river has to turn north through ninety degrees to escape.

Souther Fell is haunted, so they say, by ghostly armies. These were first seen on Midsummer's Eve 1735, exercising on top of the fell. They were seen again by a Mr Wilton and his servant in 1743, and then on Midsummer's Eve 1745, quite a lot of people saw the army, complete with gun carriages. This is the supernatural carried to excess, and nobody has ever offered a satisfactory explanation of the phenomenon, though it has been suggested it was some kind of mirage. As far as I am aware nobody has seen the Souther Fell armies for the last two hundred years, so it is likely to remain a mystery. The celebrated Lakeland painter, W. Heaton Cooper, has suggested that the apparitions might go back into ancient times and that is why the principal fell is called Blencathra, 'the hill of the devils'.

Over the col the track leads into a most attractive little cirque called Mousthwaite Comb, then round the shoulder of the fell to the main road near Scales. It is just over a mile along the road back to the car, and though there are alternative footpaths, somewhat longer, via Guardhouse and Threlkeld Hall, these are an anticlimax.

Scales Tarn and Sharp Edge.
(Photo: Duncan Unsworth).

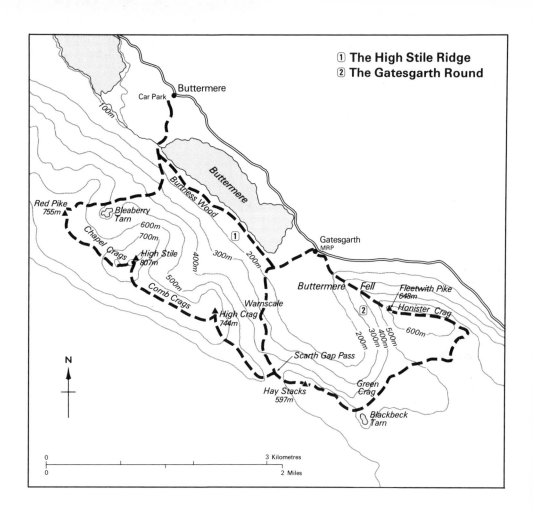

The High Stile Ridge
The Gatesgarth Round

Buttermere

Car Park

Buttermere

Burtness Wood

Red Pike
755m

Bleaberry
Tarn

600m
700m

Chapel Crags

High Stile
807m

400m

300m

200m

Gatesgarth
MRP

Comb Crags

500m

Warnscale

Buttermere   Fell

Fleetwith Pike
648m

Honister Crag

High Crag
744m

200m
300m
400m
500m
600m

N

Scarth Gap Pass

Green
Crag

Hay Stacks
597m

Blackbeck
Tarn

0   3 Kilometres
0   2 Miles

WALK 33: The High Stile Ridge

Map: English Lakes (NW) 1:25,000.
Start: MR174169. The car park in Buttermere village.
Distance: 6¹/₂ miles (10km).
Time: 6 hrs.
What's it Like?: A fine, fairly short ridge walk regarded as a classic of its kind. The ascent to Red Pike is a hard slog. The descent of Gamlin End requires caution. Surprisingly energetic; you'll know you've been for a walk.
Links with other Walks: At Scarth Gap this walk can be linked to Walk 34. A very tiring day—make sure you are up to it!
Shorter Alternatives: (1) Walk around the lake, through Burtness Wood to Gatesgarth, then back along the other shore (passing through a tunnel *en route!*): one of the best low-level walks in the Lakes—4 miles, 2 hrs—including an ice cream at Gatesgarth! (2) From Buttermere via Scale Bridge to Scale Force (MR151161). Traditionally the highest waterfall in the district at 125ft (38m), Scale Force was a set-piece attraction for the Victorians who sensibly visited it by boat across Crummock Water—it cost one shilling (5p). This option is no longer available, unfortunately, and it now involves four miles of boggy walking. As Scale Force does not readily reveal itself, being very deeply set in the fellside, this is a connoisseur's walk, suitable only for the person who has seen everything else. 3 hrs.
Bad Weather Alternatives: You could visit Sellafield—now there's a thought.

Above: **The classic view of Buttermere seen on the approach to Red Pike.**

From Buttermere Along a Classic Ridge

Of all Lakeland's popular centres Buttermere is the smallest and most awkward to reach, being attainable only by narrow roads over steep passes or along Lorton Vale. Yet this doesn't daunt the modern traveller; Buttermere on a Bank Holiday seems only slightly less

crowded than Blackpool, and car parking can be a problem. The reason for this popularity is simple: Buttermere is Lakeland at its prettiest. Not the savage grandeur that you get in Wasdale, or the sublime landscape of Borrowdale, but undeniably pretty. There are two lakes within touching distance and a third not too far away, there are fine woods, and there is a magnificent mountain ridge.

The ridge is perhaps the simplest in the Lake District to describe. It consists of three peaks—one at each end and one in the middle—and is pretty well straight, roughly north-west to south-east. It is about 2 miles (3km) long, not counting the approaches and descent, which double the distance—and they are all rough miles. The other side of the ridge is Ennerdale, where the slopes are smoothly boring, but on the Buttermere side the ridge has two great corries, plucked out by glaciers long ago. So on this side it is very steep, with lots of crags.

A broad bridle-path, well signposted, leads out of the village, past the Fish Inn, towards the waterfall of Sour Milk Gill, which can be seen clearly tumbling down the dark fellside, like a silver ribbon. A slight diversion from this path to the lake shore gives a view along the lake to Fleetwith Pike, one of Lakeland's classic views.

The bridleway ends at a bridge and divides into various paths, all of which are clearly marked. We want 'Red Pike' and so follow this into the woods which fringe the lake shore. This is Burtness Woods and many of the pines in it have now reached maturity and are being felled. They are to be replaced by oak. Soon the path divides and this is the point to which we shall eventually return, but in the meantime we take the upwards path. And upwards it certainly is. Although the path has been heavily restored and is much less fatiguing than it was, it is still a very steep ascent.

After a while the path bends sharply to the right, reaches its maximum steepness, then becomes much more gradual as it contours across the fell towards the top of Sour Milk Gill. It crosses the gill and follows it up into the corrie where lies the sombre Bleaberry Tarn. High Stile towers over the corrie, with the

Climbers on Grey Crag, High Stile. Honister Pass can be seen in the background.

The well-made path through Burtness Wood to Red Pike. (Photo: Duncan Unsworth).

broken rocks of Chapel Crags and the long nobbly ridge leading to Red Pike. Red Pike itself seems very close—and very red, for the syenite rock of which the mountain is made has a distinct ruddy colour, like burnt brick. The path climbs very steeply up this, to end at the summit, a small, grassy belvedere (2477ft/755m).

The view is extensive. Five lakes can be seen from here; Buttermere, Derwent Water, Ennerdale Water, Loweswater and Crummock Water, while to the north the great mass of the Grasmoor fells lies across the horizon like a stranded whale. In the opposite direction is dark Ennerdale and Pillar, with Scafell in the distance.

A broad ridge runs away from Red Pike to High Stile, undulating slightly, the path crossing patches of broken rocks which can twist the ankle of the unwary. It rises through broken rocks to the summit (2648ft/807m).

High Stile actually sticks out from the ridge a bit and it is easy to miss some of the best views, especially those to the east which take in Fleetwith Pike and, much nearer, a splendid profile of Grey Crag which plunges from the top of High Stile into Burtness Comb. This is a favourite crag for rock-climbers, though most of the routes are easy—the harder ones are on Eagle Crag, pressed up against the head of the comb and less easily seen.

Grey Crag can also be seen to advantage from the ridge between High Stile and the next peak, High Crag (2441ft/744m), which is soon

Gatesgarth and Fleetwith Pike from the High Stile ridge. (Photo: Duncan Unsworth).

reached. From this summit the ridge drops with startling suddenness towards a subsidiary top called Seat beyond which is the col known as Scarth Gap, the usual pass from Gatesgarth in Buttermere to the youth hostel at Black Sail.

The way down is obviously very steep and it turns out to be distinctly unpleasant as well. The slope is known as Gamlin End and consists of small scree lying on a bed of hard, slippery gravel. How the scree hasn't all been rubbed away by this time is quite beyond me, but a good deal of it has, making the descent precarious. It makes you wish you had some old-fashioned clinker nails in your boots—but that would never do in these ecological times!

Gamlin End is about 500ft (150m) of purgatory, but even this comes to an end

eventually and a path leads over Seat (1845ft/ 561m), a nice little lump, then descends suddenly left in a tumble of boulders that masquerades as a path. This is extremely rough and steep and it comes as a relief to meet the main path from Scarth Gap.

All difficulty vanishes from now on. The path is well graded, repaired in places, and the descent to it from High Crag quickly fades as bad dreams do. Where it meets the valley floor there's a gate. The broad bridleway straight ahead leads to Gatesgarth farm in a few minutes, where there is an ice cream van strategically placed in season. However, by resisting temptation and turning left along the lake shore path, you can enjoy a lovely walk through Burtness Wood back to the village.

WALK 34: The Gatesgarth Round

Map: English Lakes (NW) 1:25,000.
Start: MR195150. Gatesgarth farm car park.
Distance: 5 miles (8km).
Time: 4hrs.
What's it Like?: The intimate charm of Hay Stacks and the view down Fleetwith Edge make a unique combination of attractions. In bad visibility this is a fell to be avoided because it has more crags than most. On TV recently Wainwright assured us that Hay Stacks was his favourite fell, so you don't just have to take my word for it!
Links with Other Walks: This route can be added on to Walk 33 by a strong walker—a good day out.
Shorter Alternatives: (1) Omit Fleetwith Pike, returning instead by the very good track along Warnscale Beck, which also leads direct to Gatesgarth—saves less than an hour and you miss the glorious Fleetwith Edge view; (2) On a fitful day, when the clouds are shredding themselves amongst the crags, the walk into Warn-scale Bottom can be thrillingly sombre. One expects the Valkyries to arrive at any moment . . . About an hour, there and back.
Bad Weather Alternatives: Go for the city lights of Keswick—anywhere seems like a city after Buttermere.

A Traverse of Hay Stacks and Fleetwith Pike

At the head of Buttermere, between Ennerdale and Honister Pass, is a large tract of moorland which for the most part is quite without interest. To the south-east this land rises to two undistinguished summits, Brandreth and Grey Knotts which are seldom climbed except *en route* to somewhere else. It is the north-west fringe of the moor which excites attention; two rocky spurs around a central hollow. The more southerly of the two is called Hay Stacks,

Above: **Hay Stacks rising above Scarth Gap, with Warnscale Bottom on the left. From High Crag the Gatesgarth round can be seen in its entirety.**

Right: **Fleetwith Edge, the long west ridge of Fleetwith Pike, drops as straight as a beggar can spit into Gatesgarth. Buttermere, Crummock Water and Loweswater can be seen as the eye travels along the valley. The pudding-like fell above Crummock Water is Mellbreak.** (Photo: Duncan Unsworth).

which we are told means 'high rocks', and the other is the bold Fleetwith Pike.

The walk starts and ends at Gatesgarth. From the farm an obvious track leads across the water meadows at the head of Buttermere towards Scarth Gap. The path, nicely reconditioned in parts, climbs steeply up the fellside below High Crag, then levels out a bit and makes a more sedate ascent to the col from where there are views down to the grim-visaged Ennerdale Forest and across to the crags of Pillar. Just below here there is the Black Sail Hut, described by the Youth Hostel Association as 'the most isolated and excitingly situated hostel in England', which holds just 19 people and is closed during winter. It was formerly a shepherd's bothy.

The col is a crossroads and we take the path which slants towards Hay Stacks and leads to a scree slope and steepish ascent of the rocky fell. The summit lies almost immediately above (1959ft/597m).

The summit of Hay Stacks is a remarkable place of pools and rock outcrops; a lumpy place which has all the appearance of being rather badly assembled. There are no grand profiles here—none of your Gables or Pillar ostentation—but rather a rocky maze around which you can scramble at will. One such scramble is out onto Big Stack, a buttress which thrusts out over Warnscale Bottom and gives fine views of that wild valley head.

There are various ways round the rim of the corrie, but the main path traverses the tops to Innominate Tarn, then descends a ledge above a gully to the larger Blackbeck Tarn. Alternatively, there's a more exciting traverse along the edge of the crags, though this does miss out the lovely views around Innominate Tarn. You pays yer money and takes yer choice—except that you need to have great care when approaching the crags, and this alternative route is not an option one would take in poor weather. In fine weather, however, a diversion out to Green Crag (1733ft/528m) should be made in order to appreciate fully the majesty of the surrounding rocks.

Before long Warnscale Beck is met with, draining the wide saucer of moor round about. The main path descends by the stream back to Gatesgarth, but our route turns slightly right, past the climbing club hut and the quarries, towards the rim of the saucer which is here the crest line of Honister Crag. There is no hint in the approach of the enormous craggy face which Honister exhibits on its far side!

With luck you'll pick up a track which skirts past two small quarries and climbs to the top

of Fleetwith Pike (2126ft/648m), though a more direct ascent is possible for those who are impatient and unappreciative of the aesthetics of the thing. The view of the Buttermere fells, Pillar, Gable and Kirk Fell are impressive, seeming to crowd in on the viewer, whilst away to the north is the sprawling mass of the Coledale heights.

But perhaps more impressive than the fells even, is the view along the Buttermere valley. From the summit of Fleetwith Pike a long, narrow ridge known as Fleetwith Edge plunges down 'as straight as a beggar can spit', as Kipling might have said, leading the eye on past Buttermere and Crummock Water to Mellbreak and Loweswater.

There's a path down the ridge so that the descent—for a good way at least—is faced by this superb valley view. Down and down, in steep steps as the ridge roller-coasts to the valley. Near the bottom the path turns off right at the rock outcrop of Low Raven Crag where a hundred years ago a serving wench called Fanny Mercer was accidentally killed on her day off; a sad incident which is responsible for the conspicuous white cross let into the rock.

It is only a matter of minutes now, down to the road and back to Gatesgarth with its ice cream van.

Innominate Tarn on Hay Stacks with Great Gable in the background. (Photo: Duncan Unsworth).

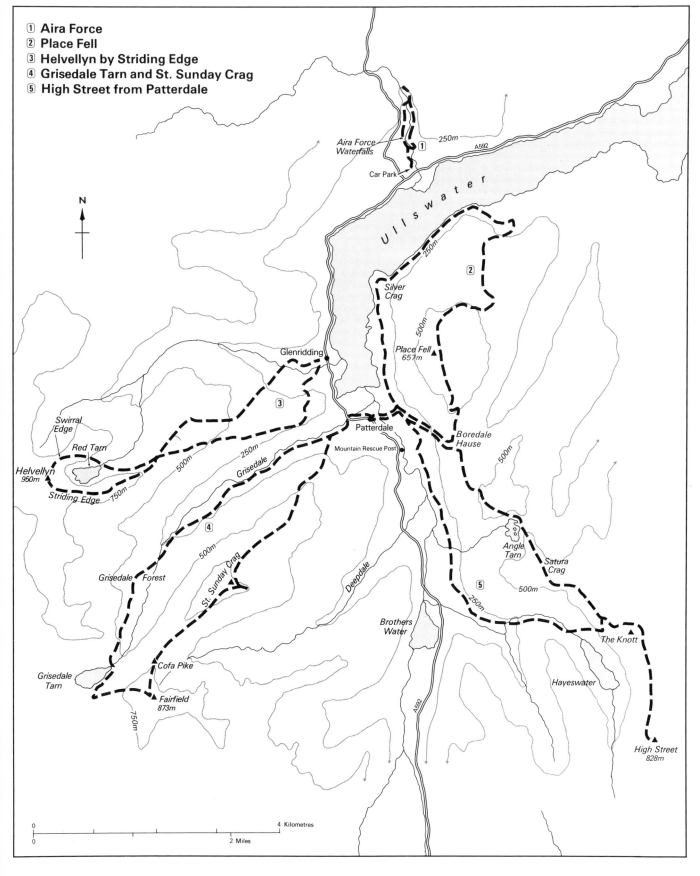

1. Aira Force
2. Place Fell
3. Helvellyn by Striding Edge
4. Grisedale Tarn and St. Sunday Crag
5. High Street from Patterdale

N

Aira Force Waterfalls
250m
A592
①
Car Park

Ullswater
250m

Silver Crag
500m
②

Place Fell 657m

Glenridding

Swirral Edge
Red Tarn
③
Patterdale
Boredale Hause
Helvellyn 950m
Striding Edge
750m
500m
Mountain Rescue Post
500m

Grisedale
250m
④
500m

Angle Tarn
Satura Crag

Grisedale Forest
St. Sunday Crag
⑤
500m
250m

Deepdale
The Knott

Brothers Water
Hayeswater

Grisedale Tarn
Cofa Pike
750m
Fairfield 873m
A592
High Street 828m

0 _____ 4 Kilometres
0 _____ 2 Miles

WALK 35: Helvellyn by Striding Edge

Map: English Lakes (NE) 1:25,000
Start: MR387169. Glenridding car park; or MR394161. Patterdale.
Distance: 7 miles (11km). Perhaps 1/4 mile more from Patterdale and add about 3/4 mile to include Catstye Cam.
Time: 5hrs.
What's it Like?: One of the great ridge walks of Britain, comparable in grandeur with Crib Goch on Snowdon. In summer no technical difficulty, but steadiness needed. Very popular and likely to be crowded. In winter this is a serious expedition needing winter equipment—ice axe and possibly crampons, and the knowledge of how to use them properly.
Shorter Alternatives: To Lanty's Tarn from Glenridding and climb Keldas (1020ft/311m). Good viewpoint for Ullswater. Possible to complete the circuit by descending to Grisedale and along the lake shore, but not as fine and there's a chance you'll get knocked down by a motorist, especially on Sunday. Best go back the same way. The whole thing could take an hour if you tried.
See also Walks 8, 36-38.
Bad Weather Alternative: See Walks 8, 36-38.

The Most Famous Ridge in the Lake District

Just as all rock-climbers must one day climb Napes Needle and all mountaineers must one day climb the Matterhorn, so all fellwalkers must eventually come face to face with Striding Edge. It is expected of them: a sort of passport without which their qualifications are regarded as somewhat dubious.

It isn't difficult to see why this ridge on Helvellyn has gained such distinction and why it is held so dear in the fellwalker's affections. It is because it is so clearcut a route, arrowlike in its directness, along a ridge which is rocky

Above: **Winter on the fells. Striding Edge lies below, quite distinct, and in the background is High Street.**

Above left: **Climbers kicking steps up the summit slopes to Helvellyn. In summer this part is loose scree.**

Above right: **Some idea of the steepness of the summit slopes can be gained from this photograph looking down on two climbers.**

and narrow. There's exposure here, and a frisson of danger—perhaps more apparent than real, though people have been killed. In my young days it was considered the ultimate in Lakeland fellwalking, and I was thought a heretic when I pointed out that Sharp Edge on Blencathra is technically harder. Jack's Rake on Pavey Ark is harder still, of course, but in those days that was considered to be rock-climbing!

Striding Edge demands a clear day, a clear head, and common sense. It is not technically difficult but neither is it a place to fool around. In mist the ridge is not difficult to follow but you lose the sense of exposure which is what it is all about, and crossing the mountain after the ridge can be tricky unless your navigation is good. In winter the ridge is absolutely magnificent and I have chosen to illustrate it with some winter pictures in this book, but *in winter conditions like those shown here Striding Edge is a mountaineering expedition requiring the right equipment and skill in using it.*

The traditional ascent of the ridge begins in Grisedale, about half a mile from the entrance to the valley. Until quite recently it was possible to park a car here but that is no longer the case so any vehicle must be parked in Patterdale or Glenridding. There's a large car park at the latter place and the walk over Keldas by Lanty's Tarn is an attractive introduction. From Patterdale the way is along

the valley road until the obvious turn-off over the bridge and up to Birkhouse Moor can be made.

Beyond the gate by Brownends Plantation the real work begins in earnest. A track slopes across the steep fellside to a place on the ridge above known as the Hole in the Wall. This ascent lasts for about a mile and a half, but it seems to go on forever; a relentless trudge whose only saving grace is the fine view it affords of Grisedale. The Hole in the Wall is just that; a gap in the remarkable drystone wall which runs for miles across the summit of Birkhouse Moor and encloses the whole southern side of the fell.

It is here that the ridge begins; a series of rocky humps crossed or avoided by well-known tracks as the case may be. Steep slopes fall away on either hand but the exposure is not really that bad until the final narrow rocky crest is reached. This is the real Striding Edge and you need to be careful, especially at the end where there's a scramble down to safer ground. The views round about are remarkably rocky; on the right there is Red Tarn with the East Face of Helvellyn towering over it and on the left the crags and gullies of Nethermost Cove. Anyone who only knows Helvellyn from the boringly bland slopes it presents to the western, Thirlmere, side would be amazed at the change the old lady presents on this side!

The ridge abuts against the mountain some

Left: **Striding Edge is likely to be busy on any day in summer.** (Photo: Duncan Unsworth).

The Dixon Memorial on Striding Edge commemorates a man killed here in 1858 whilst following the Patterdale hunt. (Photo: Duncan Unsworth).

The start of Striding Edge from the Hole in the Wall. (Photo: Duncan Unsworth).

way below the top so that there is a steep slope to climb. In summer this is a short, hard grind, but in winter it is positively Alpine in character and steps have to be kicked in the snow. It gives out onto a plateau across which there's a short walk to the summit cairn. Helvellyn is 3117ft (950m) and the third highest mountain in the Lakes. It is also the most popular in terms of the numbers climbing it and according to some authorities, it is the most frequently climbed mountain in Britain.

The central position of Helvellyn guarantees the wide range of the view from the top; the Lakeland fells in tumbled masses lie all about, but because Helvellyn is so high the view is more extensive than attractive. As John Ruskin pointed out many years ago, the best views are always from mountains of moderate height. Only in winter does it come into its own; then it really does remind one of Alexander Pope's immortal line about Alps upon Alps.

The mountain has no fewer than three memorials on or about its top. The first is actually on the Striding Edge ridge, near the start of the narrow bit and overlooking Nethermost Cove—tucked away so that most fellwalkers miss it. It commemorates Robert Dixon of Patterdale who was killed near this spot in 1858 whilst following the Patterdale Foxhounds. Where the ridge meets the plateau itself there's the Gough Memorial, erected in 1890 to commemorate Charles Gough, a

visitor from Manchester who, in April 1805, lost his way in a snow storm on Striding Edge and fell 600ft (180m) towards Red Tarn where his wasted body was discovered three months later, still guarded by his faithful Irish terrier, Foxey. It led to Wordsworth and Scott writing poems about the incident. The last memorial is rather different: it commemorates the fact that in December 1926, the celebrated aviator Bert Hinkler landed a plane on the summit plateau. Even more incredible, he managed to take off again without mishap!

Beyond the trig block lies the start of Swirrel Edge; a companion ridge to Striding Edge, forming the other arm of the Red Tarn corrie, but very much shorter. At first it is quite a steep descent but it soon eases and a good path slopes off down the side of the ridge towards the outflow from the tarn. It is worthwhile, though, to make a short diversion along the ridge to the peak at the end called Catstye Cam (2920ft/890m). Not only is this another peak attained at very little cost, but it also gives a good view of the east face of Helvellyn. Seen from below, Catstye Cam is a fine-shaped mountain in its own right.

The main path leads across Red Tarn Beck and back to the Hole in the Wall where our adventure began. Down the long slopes of Birkhouse Moor now, happily down a path which seemed purgatory a few hours ago, and so back to Patterdale or Glenridding.

WALK 36: Grisdale Tarn and St Sunday Crag

Map: English Lakes (NE) 1:25,000.
Start: MR395161. The climbing hut on the main road. Possible parking in front of the hut but the car park at the rear is strictly private.
Distance: 81/2 miles (14km).
Time: 41/2hrs.
What's it Like?: In fine weather this is a good introduction to the high fells. The walk up Grisedale may be thought rather long and tedious, but there is increasing interest throughout the day right to the magnificent views of Ullswater at the end. Cofa Pike can look frightening, but it is all show. In the mist, beware the many crags on Fairfield and the ridge.
Shorter Alternatives: (1) Walk to the tarn and back along the valley—especially worth doing on a fine winter's day when the crags are magnificent: normally, the tarn can be reached quite safely; 8 miles (13km), about 31/2 hrs; (2) From the tarn there's a short cut up the stony slopes straight to Deepdale Hause which cuts out Fairfield and Cofa Pike—saves a mile (11/2km) and a good bit of climbing; (3) Reverse the last part of the walk to St Sunday Crag and return the same way; 5 miles (8km), 3hrs or so.
Bad Weather Alternatives: (1) Visit Dalemain Hall; (2) Flee to the fleshpots of Ambleside, of which there are many.

Above: **Grisedale Tarn and St Sunday Crag.** (Photo: Duncan Unsworth).

The Heart of the Eastern Fells

The valleys which cut deeply into the east flanks of the Helvellyn range are splendidly wild and rocky. Longest of these valleys is Grisedale, which leads over Grisedale Hause into Grasmere by an old pack-horse way—and an ancient one at that, for *hause* derives from the old Norse word *hals*, meaning a pass. On the northern side the valley is flanked by Striding Edge and on its southern side by the most substantial of all the lateral ridges hereabouts, St Sunday Crag. The walk up the

144

Ullswater from St Sunday Crag.

valley and back over St Sunday Crag makes a simple circuit and gives one of the very best views of Ullswater. It is equally valid done the opposite way round to the one described here—indeed, there's much to be said for it—but that superb view of the lake for the final half hour of the day is not to be missed.

The outing starts from Patterdale with a short walk along the main road to Grisedale Bridge where a narrow lane leads off up the valley and is followed for half a mile or so until the tarmac ends and a broad track takes its place. The valley is wide and dotted with woods. On the right the great sweep of fell rising towards Striding Edge is scarred by the huge track leading to the Hole in the Wall, trodden by thousands of pilgrims each year, determined to do Lakeland's most famous ridge (see Walk 35).

On the left the fell seems just as steep and very rocky. Just beyond the Elmhow Plantation, a faint zig zag path can be seen in the bracken and this is the once notorious Elmhow

Zig Zags; a very direct way up St Sunday Crag, abominably steep and with absolutely nothing to recommend it. Small wonder it has long since fallen out of favour!

Further over there is a long band of broken crags which look most impressive. With luck, from the end of the Elmhow Plantation you might be able to make out a sharp ridge bounded by a deep gully. This is Pinnacle Ridge which in the last few years has become possibly the most popular scramble in Lakeland. It really is a ridge of sharp pinnacles, short but very exposed and the scrambling involved is Grade 3, which means it almost verges on rock-climbing. The celebrated Jack's Rake counts as Grade 1, so that will give you some idea of what's involved in tackling Pinnacle Ridge!

Before long the path starts to climb more earnestly, towards the wild corries which tower in front and which in winter look extremely dramatic. There are some good simple gullies up there for the winter mountaineer with lots

145

The head of Grisedale with Dollywaggon Pike. (Photo: Duncan Unsworth).

of step-kicking and no technicalities. In summer, the east ridge of Nethermost Pike is the best way up—quite a dramatic ridge in its way, with a bit of a scramble, though nothing like as difficult as Pinnacle Ridge.

As the path climbs, the valley narrows until it tips over a slight lip and reveals one of the most sombre tarns in Lakeland. Grisedale Tarn is never a cheerful place. Except from the way of our approach it is surrounded by high fells—Seat Sandal, Fairfield and Dollywaggon Pike, which plunge their barren slopes straight into the dark waters. The place has a brooding atmosphere, intensified when the mists swirl round the crags.

Just before the shores of the tarn are reached there's an engraved plate set in a rock commemorating the parting between William Wordsworth and his brother John in 1805, when the latter returned to his ship, the East Indiaman *Earl of Abergavenny*. William had walked over the hause from Grasmere with him and at this solemn spot they said goodbye. Little did William know that he would never see his brother again, for the ship was lost in a storm off the coast of Dorset and John was drowned along with some 300 passengers and crew. His brother carved some memorial lines on this rock near where they parted, but erosion has worn them away and the metal plate has to suffice.

From the stepping stones where the beck leaves the tarn a slanting path leads up to Grisedale Hause with a view down into the Vale of Grasmere. By turning left at the hause the stony slopes of Fairfield can be climbed to its rather smooth top (2864ft/873m). The view is more extensive than inspiring.

Fairfield is a tricky fell in misty conditions, calling for precise navigation. This is especially the case on the route we are following because the ridge towards St Sunday Crag has the sharp Cofa Pike—a spiky pimple which has to be crossed before making a steep descent to Deepdale Hause. All this section is fairly exposed, with impressive views into rocky Deepdale.

A long grassy ridge leads with elegant simplicity to the top of St Sunday Crag, which is not a crag but a mountain (2759ft/841m). The top is broad and if there is enough energy available, it is worthwhile strolling over to a secondary summit called Gavel Pike, about a quarter of a mile east, which is not only better looking in itself but also gives better views. The real view from this mountain, however, is the celebrated panorama of Ullswater and this is got by following the ridge north-east to the well-made North Cairn.

The view of lake and mountains is quite outstanding and the pleasing part is that it gets even better as you walk on along the easy ridge past the summit of Birks and down a good but steep path by Thornhow End back into Grisedale near the entrance to the valley. Not until you are well down the fellside does the view entirely vanish, though it subtly changes.

Once the road in Grisedale is reached, it is only a few minutes back to the village and the car.

WALK 37: Aira Force

Above: **'A bonny little waterspout'
– the topmost falls on the Aira
beck.** (Photo: Duncan Unsworth).

Map: English Lakes (NE) 1:25,000.
Start: MR401201. Aira Force car park.
Distance: Perhaps a little more than a mile
(1¹/₂km) from start to finish.
Time: You could rush round in twenty minutes
if you don't mind pushing old ladies out of the
way, but it is worth an hour of anybody's time,
at least.
What's it Like?: You are not likely to be lonely
on this amble, nor are you likely to get lost. You
would have to work hard to achieve either. It is
a pleasant woodland stroll, not in the least
taxing. Magnificent scenery and lots of people—
most of whom go no further than the first
bridge, thank goodness.
Bad Weather Alternatives: (1) It could be
argued that this walk *is* a bad weather alternative because the falls look especially good during a wet spell! (2) Visit Dalemain, home of the
Hasell family since 1665 and the museum of the
Westmorland and Cumberland Yeomanry. Deer
park and country life museum in grounds
(MR478269).

One of Lakeland's Finest Waterfalls

*List ye, who pass by Lyulph's Tower
At eve, how softly then
Doth Aira-force, that torrent hoarse,
Speak from the woody glen!*

So wrote Wordsworth in his gloomy poem of
love frustrated called *The Somnambulist*, in
which the medieval damsel, distressed at the
absence of her loved one at the Crusades, takes
to sleep-walking and tumbles into the torrent.
He, of course, chooses this awkward moment
to return and she lives just long enough to
recognize him. Filled with remorse he ends his
days as a hermit in a cave. Perhaps he had a
premonition about that awful third line
Wordsworth was going to write!

Aira Force is still to be found in its woody
glen on the edge of Ullswater, a few yards
down the lake from the junction where the
Matterdale road comes in. There's a wide spit

147

Right: **Aira Force, one of the best of the district's waterfalls.**

Below: **Primroses by the path to Aira Force. The woods around the beck are full of wild flowers in spring.**

of land known as Aira Point jutting into the lake just here, fringed with trees and filled with sheep. It too has its associations with Wordsworth because this is where his sister Dorothy saw the daffodils which 'seemed as if they verily laughed with the wind', as she wrote in her Journal. And we all know what that led to.

You don't have to be a Wordsworth buff to enjoy Aira Force, however. It is quite simply one of the best waterfalls in the district and the walk—scarcely more than a stroll really—is a little jewel of romantic perfection. The reason why Wordsworth chose it as the setting for his poem is readily apparent.

The Aira Beck descends through a narrow wooded dell at the western foot of Gowbarrow Fell, and in so doing forms a series of attractive falls. The property belongs to the National Trust, who care for it magnificently—not an easy job when you consider that this is one of the prime honeypot tourist sites of the Lake District. There's a fine car park, toilets and (just outwith the property) a café, and cynics might be surprised to find that the area does not seem to suffer the squalid fate one might expect. No doubt the Trust puts in a lot of hard work, but the place cannot be kept so spruce-looking without a certain amount of respect from the public.

From the car park a path leads into the woods and divides at a footbridge. It doesn't really matter which side of the stream you follow, because both lead eventually to the same place. Great trees rise from the banks and beneath their sturdy branches in spring the wild flowers grow in profusion: the primrose, oxalis and even the shy violet.

Within a few minutes the path leads to a bridge across the stream at the foot of the first waterfall, which is Aira Force itself. In wet

weather it is a roaring great spout some 60ft (18m) high and even after a dry spell it is seldom less than impressive—which is more that can be said about some waterfalls. There's a bridge above the falls to match the one below, and though it is inscribed to the memory of Stephen Edward Spring Rice—one of the Marshall family of Ullswater Hall who died in 1902—it replaced an older bridge. Thomas Allom's drawing done in the early nineteenth century shows quite clearly there were two ancient wooden bridges, one above the falls and one below.

A steep flight of steps leads up to the top bridge where there is a different view of the fall, though scarcely as fine as the one from below.

If you cross this bridge and follow the stream up you find yourself rising above it and eventually looking down on yet another waterfall, the so-called High Force, which hides itself away in a deep cleft and can't be seen properly from this viewpoint. It should be called Middle Force really, for there is yet another waterfall higher still up the beck. This has no name and no bridge, but is a bonny little waterspout for all that.

Soon after this the path leaves National Trust property, but you can follow it all the way to Dockwray if you wish, a further half-mile or so.

Instead of this, however, most visitors will want to descend to the bridge at High Force, cross it and gaze at the twin spouts pouring into the deep slot in the rocks which the water has formed over the centuries. From there it is only a matter of minutes to continue up to the third fall. Each of these three waterfalls is quite different from the others and though Aira Force itself is the most magnificent, the others are not without merit.

If you return downstream on the opposite side to that by which you ascended, until the bridge above Aira Force, you can cross this and follow a high-level path, which keeps well above the dell, back to the car park. At the place where a seat has thoughtfully been provided there is a magnificent view over Ullswater towards the head of the lake.

Some turrets of Lyulph's Tower can be seen ahead, but the Tower, built about 1780 as a shooting lodge on the site of a much older building, is privately owned by the Howard family and not open to the public. Some say that Lyulph was the first Lord of Ullswater ('Lyulph's water'), but that might be putting two and two together to make five.

The path descends steeply to the car park.

WALK 38: Place Fell

Map: English Lakes (NE) 1:25,000.
Start: MR395161. The climbing hut on the main road. Possible parking in front but the car park round the back is strictly private. There is also a car park a few yards south along the road.
Distance: 7 miles (11km).
Time: 4¹/2hrs.
What's it Like?: A neat, compact climb admirable as a first mountain for a tyro or anyone wanting to get fit. The ascent is short and fairly sharp. There's quite a bit of rock scattered about this fell so care is needed in bad weather. The return walk by the lakeshore is justifiably famous—and tougher than you might think!
Shorter Alternatives: You can use the lake steamer to cheat on this walk! Either (1) follow the first half of the walk as described, then from Scalehow Force follow the shore path to Sandwick and Howtown pier, from whence catch the steamer back to Glenridding; or (2) take the steamer to Howtown and walk back along the shore path. N.B. Both these routes are much inferior when done in reverse.
Bad Weather Alternatives: (1) Visit Dalemain, home of the Hasell family since 1665—deer park, country life museum etc (MR478269); (2) Escape to Ambleside or Penrith; (3) Go and look at Aira Force, often splendid in the rain (See Walk 37.)

A Lakeside Walk of Great Beauty

If ever there was a mountain chosen to encapsulate all that was best in Lakeland fellwalking, I think it would have to be Place Fell, that rocky eminence towering over the south-east corner of Ullswater. The fell is a perfect jewel, beautifully proportioned and splendid in isolation. The lake limits it on one side and the deep trench of Boredale on the other, and though the total area is small,

Above: **The head of Patterdale from Place Fell**. (Photo: Duncan Unsworth).

Above: **The summit of Place Fell.**
(Photo: Duncan Unsworth).

Right: **The Ullswater shore path
below Place Fell is one of the
finest scenic routes in the
Lakes.**
(Photo: Duncan Unsworth).

151

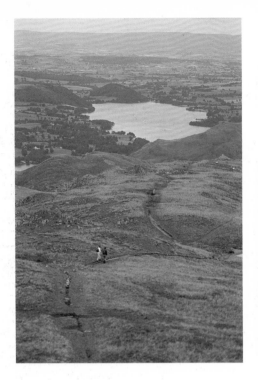

climbing the fell is never boring and where the mountain meets the lake there is a shoreline walk of incomparable loveliness.

The walk begins at the SAC hut in Patterdale and crosses the fields to the riding school at Side Farm. From behind the farm a lane leads up the valley to a cottage and gate beyond which, on the left, is another gate leading onto the fell. The next half-mile is a very steep pull up a worn path leading to Boredale Hause, but recompense comes in the ever-widening views of the upper valley, with Brothers Water and Red Screes prominent.

There is no need to go to the Hause itself for the path up Place Fell slopes off just before you arrive there and climbs more or less directly to the summit (2156ft/657m). The cairn and trig block occupy a distinct little ridge with a few small tarns scattered round about. The views are widespread in the extreme: to the east the whole length of Roman High Street can be traced from Arthur's Pike to Thornthwaite Crag, and further east still, Cross Fell and the Pennines. The Helvellyn range dominates the west and beyond the Dodds there are Skiddaw and Blencathra.

Despite the prominent right of way shown on the map, the usual way from the summit is along the little ridge then straight across to the head of Low Moss Gill. There's a good path which drops straight down the attractive little

valley formed by Scalehow Beck and then, in a graceful curve, sweeps down to join the lakeside path from Sandwick. Meanwhile the beck itself slides over a rock to form the attractive cascade of Scalehow Force.

The panorama of Ullswater revealed on the descent is merely a taste of what is to come as you make you way along the lakeside path towards Patterdale. The path, which is always good, rises and falls, skirting rocks and entering copses. It is sufficiently above the water level to give a slightly elevated view of the lake. Sailing boats tack to and fro, getting the best of the breeze, and the lake steamer chugs past, looking for all the world like the *African Queen*.

Part of the attraction lies in the fact that not all the lake can be seen at any one time. There are a couple of distinct kinks in the shape of Ullswater, and what with these and the various outcrops and contours, the view is ever-changing. Little bays appear and vanish.

Place Fell itself seems incredibly rocky when seen from the path and so it is, though not nearly as steep as it appears to be when seen from across the lake.

Eventually, the head of the lake comes in sight and the path becomes a lane servicing the camp sites. It is only a short step now to Side Farm and so back to the car.

Above left: **The view north from Place Fell. The town in the distance is Penrith.** (Photo: Duncan Unsworth).

Above right: **The path along Ullswater is a scene of constantly changing beauty.**

WALK 39: High Street from Patterdale

Brothers Water from the path to Angle Tarn. (Photo: Duncan Unsworth).

Map: English Lakes (NE) 1:25,000.
Start: MR395161. The climbing hut on the main road. Possible parking in front of hut (car park at rear strictly private) or there is a car park a few yards south along the road.
Distance: 11 miles (18km).
Time: 5hrs.
What's it Like?: An extremely scenic walk; pointless in bad weather because it is long and quite tiring, and in any case High Street is a confusing and dangerous fell in poor visibility. Good navigation required or you could end up a very long way from home! Between Angle Tarn and the Knott the path can be boggy.
N.B. The rescue box on Knott (see text) may shortly be removed.
Shorter Alternatives: (1) To Angle Tarn and back—safe and scenic, 2hrs; (2) To Hartsop and back along the valley paths, 2hrs; (3) From Hartsop to Hayeswater and back, 1¹/2hrs. There are many more alternatives in this valley. See Walks 36, 37 and 38.

Bad Weather Alternatives: (1) Visit Dalemain, home of the Hasell family since 1665—deer park and country life museum (MR478269); (2) Drive over Kirkstone to Ambleside or Grasmere and sample their various attractions.

Lost Valleys and High Tarns in a Walk of Rare Beauty

I don't think anyone in the know would argue with the proposition that High Street's summit is fairly undistinguished. It is a small plateau (the local farmers used to hold horse races there) with a broken wall and concrete trig block and absolutely nothing else. And yet it is seminal to walking in the eastern fells, because the routes up and around it are truly magnificent. This is a case where the journey is everything and the goal of little account.

The route from Patterdale is quite long, but combined with a descent by the 'ordinary'

route to Hartsop it makes an extremely fine circuit. It is a walk for views, so you need to choose a clear day.

The walk begins by the side of the ABMSAC climbing hut at Patterdale, easily recognized by its crest on the door, and follows a broad path over the river and across the fields to the riding school at Side Farm. Round the back of the farm the bridleway continues to a pretty cottage where a gate leads, surprisingly, onto a stretch of tarmac road. This really doesn't concern us so we turn off it through another gate and onto a steep path leading up the fell. (N.B. This is the same start as for Walk 38).

The path climbs steeply, divides in two—we take the lower one—and continues remorselessly to Boredale Hause; a flatish area which is the pass over into Boredale. If you are feeling energetic you can wander over to the eastern edge of the pass and look down into this remote valley. There's a good backwards view of Ullswater, too, and as you climb up towards Angle Tarn the views are continually fine,

especially at the head of Dubhow Beck where the bed of the gill funnels the eye down towards Brothers Water, Red Screes and the Dodds. Then the path climbs round a shoulder of Angletarn Pikes and you catch your first glimpse of the tarn itself; reckoned by many to be the loveliest in Lakeland.

That's as maybe—but nobody can deny that Angle Tarn, with its tiny islets and its high, remote setting, is a perfect jewel. It is quite a large tarn too, reed fringed and on the western bank made more impressive by Cat Crag whose rocks plunge straight into the water.

I once saw a walker calmly having lunch on one of the islets. How did he get there? They are too far from the shore to jump across, and surely it wasn't worth wading out? It might even be too deep for that. Levitation seems the only answer!

There's another climb now, up to Satura Crag, passing another tarn on the way—but a small one, not even marked on the map. To the north there is a glimpse of Bannerdale, a valley

Angle Tarn, regarded by many as the prettiest in Lakeland.

The Straits of Riggindale from High Street.

which is even more remote than Boredale, but to the south the views are of deepset Hayeswater and the High Street range. The path, which has been pretty fair until now, has become excessively boggy in places and it remains so, on and off, for the next mile.

As the path rises to go round the Knott, a dome-like hill, there are fine views east to the impressive rocks of Rampsgill Head which from this distance deceive the eye into believing they are a major climbing crag. There's even a smaller version of Pillar Rock, or so it seems . . .

Just round the corner, on the Knott, there is a big blue Mountain Rescue box—not too obtrusive, I think, and a useful landmark if you're navigating through the mist! Beyond this point the path tackles a short narrow ridge called the Straits of Riggindale, the name of which is more impressive than the ridge itself. It is, however, the gate to High Street and the path, now broadly generous, sweeps away over the gentle plateau.

Don't follow it! High Street is probably the only major fell where the path avoids the summit altogether. It is better to follow the broken wall (where another path is developing in its own right) which will lead directly to the trig point, or follow the eastern edge of the mountain, with its superb views down Riggindale and Blea Water to Haweswater. This wonderful view is a fitting climax to the walk.

The return journey retraces our steps for about a mile, until just beyond the blue rescue box on the Knott, where a clear path zig zags down the steep slopes to Hayeswater Gill. There are paths on each bank of the stream and both lead into the attractive hamlet of Hartsop, with its seventeenth-century houses, huddled together in haphazard fashion. Two of them—Low House and Thorn House—retain their original open spinning galleries.

Just beyond the houses a bridleway leads off the road to the right and provides a gentle valley walk of rather more than two miles back to the car.

WALK 40: Caldbeck and the Howk

Map: The most suitable map is a sketch map found in the pamphlet *Short Walks Around Caldbeck Village*, produced by the Local History Society and available in the village for a few pence. I am indebted to this pamphlet and the delightful booklet *Caldbeck* by Maureen Allen for much of the historical information in this chapter.

Start: MR322399. The car park on the edge of the village by the B5299.

Distance: Little more than a mile (1½km).

Time: Not really applicable, but allow 3hrs for a good potter around.

What's it like?: The Howk path can be muddy after rain, otherwise the walk is level and easy. A very pretty village with absorbing social and industrial interest.

Bad Weather Alternatives: The church and the Priest's Mill complex offer shelter from the rain. Excellent café and antiquarian bookshop at the latter.

A Walk Round John Peel's Village

Any book of Lakeland walks must concern itself mainly with the high fells because that is what the district is mostly about; but not entirely. Some of the towns and villages are worth exploring intimately for they are full of fascinating vernacular architecture and rich in historical associations; and none more so than Caldbeck, a large village at the extreme northern edge of the area, beyond Skiddaw, and famous as the birthplace of John Peel.

The village is situated at the junction of two swift streams, the Cald Beck and Gill Beck which provided power for early corn mills and the later industrial mills. Between 1800 and 1880 there were no fewer than eight working mills in this village! In addition there was considerable mining activity in the hills above—for lead, copper, silver and barytes—

Above: **In the gorge of the Howk, Caldbeck.** (Photo: Duncan Unsworth).

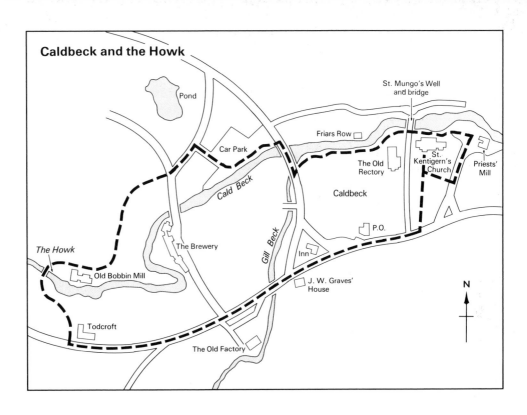

Caldbeck and the Howk

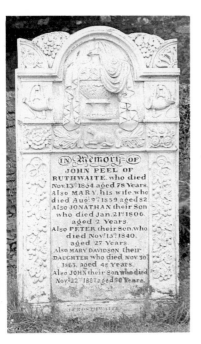

John Peel's grave, Caldbeck churchyard. (Photo: Duncan Unsworth).

as well as coal in Ratten Row, just beyond the village pond. The last mine, Potts Gill, was a barytes mine which closed as recently as 1965.

All this early industry made Caldbeck a very prosperous village and this is still reflected in the buildings and general appearance of the place.

The walk starts at the commodious car park on the north side of the village, near where the two streams meet. The steep slopes above the car park were a tenter—a place where posts with hooks, known as tenterhooks, were placed so that wool cloth could be stretched and dried, after it had been walked or fulled (the process of cleaning and shrinking the cloth once it was woven). The cloth was hung up to dry in lengths—a length being 21 yards long and 3 yards wide; a day's work.

Following the exit road from the car park leads to the village green and pond, on the far side of which is the area called Ratten Row, where until almost the middle of the last century there was Caldbeck Colliery, a small pit providing local fuel.

Leaving the pond and its attendant ducks, and turning west along the road brings you to one of Caldbeck's finest groups of buildings. The Cald Beck flows under a bridge on the far side of which is a complex of old mill buildings. Nearest the bridge is the small Lord's Mill, a corn mill belonging to the lord of the manor

where all corn had to be ground. It was a manorial mill until 1914. Beyond it is the larger brewery, with its squat chimney, which ceased to function about the turn of the century. Before it was a brewery it was a wheat mill, and one of the doors has a date stone of 1671. The two mills shared a long mill race, the tail of which can be seen from the bridge. The buildings were fortunate in never being allowed to become derelict and now they have been converted into attractive dwellings. The house across the road from the brewery became the rectory in 1984 when the old rectory was sold.

A short distance back fom the bridge there is the corner of an old building which bears the sign 'Footpath to the Howk' and invites the traveller to step through a sort of postern gate into an ancient and decrepit yard from where a muddy bridleway leads into the woods. The stream and the path come closer together as both penetrate into a deep limestone gorge. A howk is a scooping out, which is what the rushing water of the Cald Beck has done here. It is short, sharp and spectacular; unusual in that the beck is a perfectly normal moorland stream above and below the Howk, but for a few hundred yards it goes berserk, carving a fantastic gorge like a miniature Cheddar down which it leaps in spectacular bounds.

In itself the Howk would be just a pretty

little glen, but incredibly, in 1857, a bobbin mill was built at the entrance to the gorge, powered by an enormous 42ft (13m) diameter water wheel named Auld Red Rover; the largest in the country at that time. The mill made bobbins for the textile mills, diversifying at times into other lathe-turned articles such as rolling pins. The mill closed about 1920, but the great wheel survived until 1940 when, like much fine ironwork, it was scrapped to provide metal for the war effort. Most of the iron proved quite unsuitable and was never used.

In earlier days there was a natural limestone bridge—a 'God's bridge'—across the Howk, but this was blown up by an irate farmer in a dispute over rights of way. Today there is a smart wooden bridge from which to see the waterfalls.

Across the bridge the way gives into an open field and though there is no path, the route lies directly across to the farm which can be seen on the other side. There is a stile on the right, giving access to the main road. The curious rows of pedestals at the side of the farm, which look like something left over from Hadrian's Wall, are old staddle stones which were used to keep the corn stooks off the ground and out of the reach of rats.

This ancient farmhouse is Todcrofts, traditional home of the Harrisons, and the place where Mary, the Maid of Buttermere, ended her days as the wife of Richard Harrison. She was a famous beauty, praised by the Lake

Above left: **The ruined bobbin mill at the entrance to the Howk, Caldbeck.**

Above right: **Caldbeck church and the steps leading down to St Mungo's Well.**

Above left: **Friar's Row, Caldbeck.**

Above right: **The Howk.**

Below: **The restored water wheel at the Priest's Mill, Caldbeck.**

Poets, and duped into marriage by a rogue named Hope who turned out to be married already. He was hanged at Carlisle in 1803. Mary's story has been dramatized several times, most recently by Melvyn Bragg, who is himself from the area. She is buried in Caldbeck churchyard.

Along the main road towards the village centre, the first houses are known as Gatesbridge, set down in a hollow. A modern steelyard is behind them but behind that is an old mill, now much altered, known as the Old Factory, where grey homespun cloth was made using undyed Herdwick wool. The first tenant was John Woodcock Graves, who lived at Gate House, just beyond the Gill Beck. It was at Gate House that Graves composed the song 'D'ye Ken John Peel', in honour of the famous huntsman. John Peel's coat was 'grey' not 'gay' as is sometimes sung—the grey cloth which came from Graves' factory.

The road passes over the Gill Beck where there is yet another old mill, now a clogger's shop, and then past Graves' house and the pub to the gates of a very handsome house, built as a rectory in 1785 but sold by the church in 1984. There are some fine Gothic windows in the side facing the churchyard.

The church is next to the old rectory. It was built in the middle of the twelfth century and is dedicated to St Kentigern, also known as St Mungo, though it is likely there was once an earlier church on the site. St Mungo preached here about 553 AD and is supposed to have used the well behind the church for baptising converts.

In the churchyard, on the west side near a small gate, are the gravestones of John Peel and Mary Richardson (The Maid of Buttermere). Peel's gravestone is white and easily spotted but Mary's is not so obvious.

The walk goes out of the churchyard by a gate in the east wall, where a short lane leads down to the Priest's Mill on the Cald Beck. Built by the rector in 1702 for grinding corn it served until the 1930s when it became a sawmill. It was disused from 1967 to 1985 when it was beautifully restored to make a café and a number of small shops. The mill wheel turns again and can best be seen from a bridge over the river, behind the café.

From the mill there's a footpath along the river bank to a small bridge, Church Bridge. We don't cross the bridge but instead go down steps beyond it to the river bank again, where there is St Mungo's Well, a shallow trough in which the water still bubbles as it has done for almost 1500 years. Across the beck lie the attractive cottages of Friar's Row and Friar Hall where at one time there was another fulling mill, now gone. In summer this riverside walk is extremely picturesque.

It leads back to the car park.